Layers of Learning

Year Two • Unit Nine

Crusades
Balkans
Digestive & Senses
Religious Art

Published by HooDoo Publishing
United States of America
© 2014 Layers of Learning
Copies of maps or activities may be made for a particular family or classroom.
ISBN 978-1495305078

If you wish to reproduce or print excerpts of this publication, please contact us at contact@layers-of-learning.com for permission. Thank you for respecting copyright laws.

Units At A Glance: Topics For All Four Years of the Layers of Learning Program

1	History	Geography	Science	The Arts
1	Mesopotamia	Maps & Globes	Planets	Cave Paintings
2	Egypt	Map Keys	Stars	Egyptian Art
3	Europe	Global Grids	Earth & Moon	Crafts
4	Ancient Greece	Wonders	Satellites	Greek Art
5	Babylon	Mapping People	Humans in Space	Poetry
6	The Levant	Physical Earth	Laws of Motion	List Poems
7	Phoenicians	Oceans	Motion	Moral Stories
8	Assyrians	Deserts	Fluids	Rhythm
9	Persians	Arctic	Waves	Melody
10	Ancient China	Forests	Machines	Chinese Art
11	Early Japan	Mountains	States of Matter	Line & Shape
12	Arabia	Rivers & Lakes	Atoms	Color & Value
13	Ancient India	Grasslands	Elements	Texture & Form
14	Ancient Africa	Africa	Bonding	African Tales
15	First North Americans	North America	Salts	Creative Kids
16	Ancient South America	South America	Plants	South American Art
17	Celts	Europe	Flowering Plants	Jewelry
18	Roman Republic	Asia	Trees	Roman Art
19	Christianity	Australia & Oceania	Simple Plants	Instruments
20	Roman Empire	You Explore	Fungi	Composing Music

2	History	Geography	Science	The Arts
1	Byzantines	Turkey	Climate & Seasons	Byzantine Art
2	Barbarians	Ireland	Forecasting	Illumination
3	Islam	Arabian Peninsula	Clouds & Precipitation	Creative Kids
4	Vikings	Norway	Special Effects	Viking Art
5	Anglo Saxons	Britain	Wild Weather	King Arthur Tales
6	Charlemagne	France	Cells and DNA	Carolingian Art
7	Normans	Nigeria	Skeletons	Canterbury Tales
8	Feudal System	Germany	Muscles, Skin, & Cardiopulmonary	Gothic Art
9	Crusades	Balkans	Digestive & Senses	Religious Art
10	Burgundy, Venice, Spain	Switzerland	Nerves	Oil Paints
11	Wars of the Roses	Russia	Health	Minstrels & Plays
12	Eastern Europe	Hungary	Metals	Printmaking
13	African Kingdoms	Mali	Carbon Chem	Textiles
14	Asian Kingdoms	Southeast Asia	Non-metals	Vivid Language
15	Mongols	Caucasus	Gases	Fun With Poetry
16	Medieval China & Japan	China	Electricity	Asian Arts
17	Pacific Peoples	Micronesia	Circuits	Arts of the Islands
18	American Peoples	Canada	Technology	Indian Legends
19	The Renaissance	Italy	Magnetism	Renaissance Art I
20	Explorers	Caribbean Sea	Motors	Renaissance Art II

3	History	Geography	Science	The Arts
1	Age of Exploration	Argentina and Chile	Classification & Insects	Fairy Tales
2	The Ottoman Empire	Egypt and Libya	Reptiles & Amphibians	Poetry
3	Mogul Empire	Pakistan & Afghanistan	Fish	Mogul Arts
4	Reformation	Angola & Zambia	Birds	Reformation Art
5	Renaissance England	Tanzania & Kenya	Mammals & Primates	Shakespeare
6	Thirty Years' War	Spain	Sound	Baroque Music
7	The Dutch	Netherlands	Light & Optics	Baroque Art I
8	France	Indonesia	Bending Light	Baroque Art II
9	The Enlightenment	Korean Pen.	Color	Art Journaling
10	Russia & Prussia	Central Asia	History of Science	Watercolors
11	Conquistadors	Baltic States	Igneous Rocks	Creative Kids
12	Settlers	Peru & Bolivia	Sedimentary Rocks	Native American Art
13	13 Colonies	Central America	Metamorphic Rocks	Settler Sayings
14	Slave Trade	Brazil	Gems & Minerals	Colonial Art
15	The South Pacific	Australasia	Fossils	Principles of Art
16	The British in India	India	Chemical Reactions	Classical Music
17	Boston Tea Party	Japan	Reversible Reactions	Folk Music
18	Founding Fathers	Iran	Compounds & Solutions	Rococo
19	Declaring Independence	Samoa and Tonga	Oxidation & Reduction	Creative Crafts I
20	The American Revolution	South Africa	Acids & Bases	Creative Crafts II

4	History	Geography	Science	The Arts
1	American Government	USA	Heat & Temperature	Patriotic Music
2	Expanding Nation	Pacific States	Motors & Engines	Tall Tales
3	Industrial Revolution	U.S. Landscapes	Energy	Romantic Art I
4	Revolutions	Mountain West States	Energy Sources	Romantic Art II
5	Africa	U.S. Political Maps	Energy Conversion	Impressionism I
6	The West	Southwest States	Earth Structure	Impressionism II
7	Civil War	National Parks	Plate Tectonics	Post-Impressionism
8	World War I	Plains States	Earthquakes	Expressionism
9	Totalitarianism	U.S. Economics	Volcanoes	Abstract Art
10	Great Depression	Heartland States	Mountain Building	Kinds of Art
11	World War II	Symbols and Landmarks	Chemistry of Air & Water	War Art
12	Modern East Asia	The South States	Food Chemistry	Modern Art
13	India's Independence	People of America	Industry	Pop Art
14	Israel	Appalachian States	Chemistry of Farming	Modern Music
15	Cold War	U.S. Territories	Chemistry of Medicine	Free Verse
16	Vietnam War	Atlantic States	Food Chains	Photography
17	Latin America	New England States	Animal Groups	Latin American Art
18	Civil Rights	Home State Study	Instincts	Theater & Film
19	Technology	Home State Study II	Habitats	Architecture
20	Terrorism	America in Review	Conservation	Creative Kids

www.layers-of-learning.com

Unit 2-9 Printable Pack

This unit includes printables at the end. To make life easier for you we also created digital printable packs for each unit. To retrieve your printable pack for Unit 2-9, please visit

www.layers-of-learning.com/digital-printable-packs/

Put the printable pack in your shopping cart and use this coupon code:

5543UNIT2-9

Your printable pack will be free.

LAYERS OF LEARNING INTRODUCTION

This is part of a series of units in the Layers of Learning homeschool curriculum, including the subjects of history, geography, science, and the arts. Children from 1st through 12th can participate in the same curriculum at the same time -family school style.

The units are intended to be used in order as the basis of a complete curriculum (once you add in a systematic math, reading, and writing program). You begin with Year 1 Unit 1 no matter what ages your children are. Spend about 2 weeks on each unit. You pick and choose the activities within the unit that appeal to you and read the books from the book list that are available to you or find others on the same topic from your library. We highly recommend that you use the timeline in every history section as the backbone. Then flesh out your learning with reading and activities that highlight the topics you think are the most important.

Alternatively, you can use the units as activity ideas to supplement another curriculum in any order you wish. You can still use them with all ages of children at the same time.

When you've finished with Year One, move on to Year Two, Year Three, and Year Four. Then begin again with Year One and work your way through the years again. Now your children will be older, reading more involved books, and writing more in depth. When you have completed the sequence for the second time, you start again on it for the third and final time. If your student began with Layers of Learning in 1st grade and stayed with it all the way through she would go through the four year rotation three times, firmly cementing the information in her mind in ever increasing depth. At each level you should expect increasing amounts of outside reading and writing. High schoolers in particular should be reading extensively, and if possible, participating in discussion groups.

☺ ☺ ☺ These icons will guide you in spotting activities and books that are appropriate for the age of child you are working with. But if you think an activity is too juvenile or too difficult for your kids, adjust accordingly. The icons are not there as rules, just guides.

☺ GRADES 1-4
☺ GRADES 5-8
☺ GRADES 9-12

Within each unit we share:
- EXPLORATIONS, activities relating to the topic;
- EXPERIMENTS, usually associated with science topics;
- EXPEDITIONS, field trips;
- EXPLANATIONS, teacher helps or educational philosophies.

In the sidebars we also include Additional Layers, Famous Folks, Fabulous Facts, On the Web, and other extra related topics that can take you off on tangents, exploring the world and your interests with a bit more freedom. The curriculum will always be there to pull you back on track when you're ready.

You can learn more about how to use this curriculum at www.layers-of-learning.com/layers-of-learning-program/

CRUSADES – BALKANS – DIGESTIVE & SENSES– RELIGIOUS ART

UNIT NINE
CRUSADES – BALKANS – DIGESTIVE & SENSES – RELIGIOUS ART

Whoever wishes to foresee the future must consult the past; for human events ever resemble those of preceding times. This arises from the fact that they are produced by men who ever have been, and ever shall be, animated by the same passions, and thus they necessarily have the same results.
-Niccolo Machiavelli

LIBRARY LIST:

HISTORY

Search for: Crusades, Black Death, plague, Richard the Lionheart, Saladin, Robin Hood Tales, St. Francis of Assisi, John Wycliffe, Jan Hus

- Make This Cathedral by Iain Ashman. A paper model to put together. There is also a town, a castle, and a crusader castle in the series.
- Plagues, Pox, and Pestilence by Richard Platt. The "bugs" are declaring war!
- Bubonic Plague by Jim Whiting.
- Saladin: Noble Prince of Islam by Diane Stanley.
- Cathedral: The Story of its Construction by David Macaulay. Incredible drawings, detailed descriptions. A really fascinating book.
- The Beggar's Bible by Louis A. Vernon. The story of John Wycliffe.
- Cathedrals and the Church by Patricia Levy.
- The Church by Kathryn Hinds.
- My Story: The Great Plague by Pamela Oldfield. Fictional diary.
- Medieval Medicine and the Plague by Lynne Elliot.
- The Door in the Wall by Marguerite de Angeli. A young boy survives the plague only to be abandoned and crippled. He must find a way to overcome his circumstances.
- Crusades by Jane Parsons. From DK.
- The Minstrel's Tale by Anna Questerly.
- Stories From the Crusades by Janet Harvey Kelman. Tales of real leaders.
- God Wills It! A Tale of the First Crusade by William Stearns Davis.
- The New Concise History of the Crusades by Thomas F. Madden. Short, not bogged down in details, great for the young student, covers all the crusades, treats the crusaders fairly, not slanted to fit with modern sensibilities.
- God's Battalions: The Case For the Crusades by Rodney Stark. Myths about the Crusades debunked. The author starts with the aggression of Islam.
- A Knight of the White Cross: A Tale of the Siege of Rhodes by G.A. Henty.
- Winning His Spurs: A Tale of the Crusades by G.A. Henty.
- Inferno by Dante. This work had a major influence on Christianity from the Middle Ages down to the present time.

Crusades – Balkans – Digestive & Senses – Religious Art

GEOGRAPHY	Search for: Balkan States, Albania, Bosnia and Herzegovina, Bulgaria, Croatia, Greece, Kosovo, Montenegro, Serbia, and Macedonia ☺ I Have an Olive Tree by Eve Bunting. A family travels to Greece to re-connect with family members. ☺ Cat From Kosovo by Mary Jane Hampton. A couple and their cat must flee war torn Kosovo. ☺ The King Has Goat Ears by Katarina Jovanovic. A fairy tale from Serbia. ☺ The Bird Maiden: A Serbian Legend by Jan M. Mike. Includes information about Serbia in the back. ☺ ☺ Stories of Hope and Spirit by Dan Keding. Folk tales told by the author's grandmother to him as a young boy. Mostly from Croatia. ☺ Zlata's Diary by Zlata Filipovic. A true diary written by a young girl who flees war torn Sarajevo in the 1990's for Paris, France. Reminded me of a modern *Diary of Anne Frank*. ☺ Dobry by Monica Shannon. A young Bulgarian boy from the early 20th century grows up to become an artist. ☺ The Day of the Pelican by Katherine Paterson. A family must flee persecution in Kosovo in the 1990's and immigrate to America.
SCIENCE	Search for: digestive system, senses, touch, sight, taste, hearing, smell ☺ My First Human Body Book by Patricia J. Wynne and Donald Silver. Coloring book. ☺ The Digestive System by Rebecca L. Johnson. ☺ The Magic School Bus Inside the Human Body by Joanna Cole. ☺ The Magic School Bus Explores the Senses by Joanna Cole. ☺ My Five Senses by Aliki. ☺ ☺ Guts: Our Digestive System by Seymour Simon. ☺ Disgusting Digestion by Nick Arnold. ☺ ☺ Cooking For Geeks: Real Science, Great Hacks, and Good Food by Jeff Potter. This book is mostly for people who are interested in cooking, but it also has fascinating sections on the science of taste. Conversational and entertaining. Sections could be read aloud to younger kids too. ☺ Human Body: An Illustrated Guide to Every Part of the Human Body and How It Works by Martyn Page, ed. From DK. Adult. Very visual, but also explanatory text. ☺ Body By Design by Allen L. Gillan. From a creationist standpoint.
THE ARTS	Search for: Gothic art, religious art, Christian art, medieval Christian art ☺ Sign and Symbols in Christian Art by George Furguson. ☺ Saints in Art by Rosa Giorgi. Images make it a good book for younger kids with an adult to guide. ☺ The Lion Companion to Christian Art by Michelle P. Brown. Covers Christian Art history from earliest times to today.

CRUSADES – BALKANS – DIGESTIVE & SENSES – RELIGIOUS ART

HISTORY: CRUSADES

Teaching Tip

Crusades, Black Death and medieval Christianity can be difficult topics to find books for the younger kids. Just keep reading about knights in armor and the Middle Ages in general.

Fabulous Fact

In the medieval Catholic Church there were secular clergy and regular clergy. Secular clergy were priests, but they did not take the same vows that the regular clergy took and they lived more in the world.

Additional Layer

While the Catholic Church always dissuaded marriage in clerics, it wasn't until the 12th century that vows of celibacy were required of all clerics. The Greek Church, on the other hand, always encouraged marriage for priests.

Learn more about some of the fundamental differences between the Greek and the Roman churches. It will shed some light on why the west was so slow to aid Constantinople.

The Christian Byzantine Empire held the Holy Land for many years, but eventually the Arab Muslims took it over when the Byzantines became weak. Still, Jews and Christians were welcome to live and do business and go on pilgrimages to Jerusalem unmolested. In fact, it was a big moneymaker in the area. It wasn't long before the Arab Muslims were overrun by the Turkish Muslims, who didn't understand the good business deal that was going down. The Turks killed the Christians and Jews and murdered pilgrims. This really made the pope angry. It also scared eastern Europeans, since they knew they were next. Constantinople had been asking for help for years, and finally, the pope decided the time for a holy war was ripe.

In a speech given in the fall of 1095, Pope Claremont called for a crusade to re-take Jerusalem, pushing back the Muslims and making the Holy City safe for Christian pilgrims. Over the next four hundred years crusades were launched, more or less successfully. Meanwhile, back home the Crusades were helping to consolidate the power of the church. The church began several militant orders and claimed that the kings of Europe derived their powers from God through the medium of the church. If you weren't crowned with the blessing of the pope, you weren't really king. Many kings fought against the growing power of the popes.

One of the militant orders, the Teutonic Knights, were used primarily to conquer new areas of eastern Europe and convert the

7

Crusades – Balkans – Digestive & Senses – Religious Art

people at the point of the sword. The inquisition in Germany was first begun during this time too. The church, once it had become linked to political power, became anxious to hang on to and expand that power by any means. Later beliefs in the separation of church and state by the American Founders grew out of past European experiences. Government can be for good and religion can be for good, but united they are quickly corrupted.

The final event that shaped these years was the Black Death, or the Plague. It swept from town to town from Asia Minor across Europe, ending in Russia in the east and Ireland in the west. Wherever it passed, thousands upon thousands were left dead. As much as 1/3 of Europe's population was wiped out by the epidemic. Such vast loses can't help but transform a people.

More Books!
We didn't have room in the book lists for Robin Hood, so here are some of our favorites.
- Robin Hood and the Golden Arrow by Robert D. San Souci
- Robin Hood by Angela Bull
- Robin Hood by Margaret Early
- The Adventures of Robin Hood by Richard Green
- Robin Hood by Paul Creswick
- Robin Hood by J.W. McSpadden
- The Adventures of Robin Hood by Howard Pyle

☺ ☺ ☺ EXPLORATION: Timeline
Printable timeline squares are at the end of this unit.
- 1065 Westminster Abbey consecrated
- November 27, 1095 Pope Urban II makes a speech calling for a crusade
- 1096-1099 First Crusade
- June 1097 Crusaders take Antioch
- July 15, 1099 Crusaders capture Jerusalem
- 1099 Knights Hospitaller founded
- 1119 Knights Templar Founded
- 1147-1149 Second Crusade
- 1163 Notre Dame Cathedral construction begun
- Oct 3, 1187 Saladin captures Jerusalem

Additional Layer
We tend to feel as though everyone at the time of the Crusades was fully on board with the concept of a religious war instigated, encouraged, and led by the church. That is not true at all. The church had debated and agonized over whether war in God's name was justified for years. On the one hand, the shedding of blood is never a good thing, but on the other hand they felt there was an obligation to protect pilgrims and stop Muslim incursions.

What do you think?

CRUSADES – BALKANS – DIGESTIVE & SENSES – RELIGIOUS ART

Additional Layer

I wish Robin Hood were real, but he probably wasn't, or at least the tales are only very loosely based on a real person. King Richard and Prince John and the Sheriff of Nottingham are very real though.

Additional Layer

In the early Middle Ages a king would appoint, or invest a bishop or cardinal of the church to an office within the king's territory. This meant the king was the spiritual head of the church within his domains. The pope didn't like the king having this power. He wanted to change it so that only the pope could appoint bishops and other high ranking church officials. This would make the church independent of the kings. The fight over this is called the Investiture Controversy. The pope won in 1122 at the Concordant of Worms.

- 1189-1192 Third Crusade
- Oct 4, 1190 Teutonic Knights founded
- 1191 King Richard I of England goes on Crusade
- July 12, 1191 Crusaders capture Acre
- Dec 11, 1191 Richard captured by a German Baron near Vienna and held for ransom
- March 3, 1193 Death of Saladin
- March 12, 1194 Richard returns to England to find John has usurped his kingdom.
- March 28, 1194 Richard captures Nottingham Castle, retaking his kingdom.
- 1201-1204 Fourth Crusade
- 1205 St. Francis of Assisi founds Franciscan order of Friars
- 1218-1221 Fifth Crusade
- 1228-1229 Sixth Crusade
- 1233 Inquisition begun in Germany
- 1248-1254 Seventh Crusade
- 1270 Eighth Crusade
- 1304 Divine Comedy written by Dante
- 1309 Knights Hospitaller take over the island of Rhodes and make it their base
- 1311 Knights Templar disbanded
- 1344 Plague in Constantinople
- 1345-1350 Plague spreads across Europe

☺ ☺ ☺ **EXPLORATION: St. George**

Many crusaders wore the red cross of St. George on a white background. St. George had been a Roman soldier born in Turkey. He was also a Christian. The most famous legend of St. George is where he slays a dragon to save a princess and a town. Later he was martyred when Emperor Diocletian found out he was a Christian and George refused to recant.

There are many versions of the tale of St. George. Check out your library to read one. Also go to the National Gallery of Art to go on a guided tour of art about St. George. http://www.nga.gov/kids/rogier/rogier1.htm

CRUSADES – BALKANS – DIGESTIVE & SENSES – RELIGIOUS ART

St. George and the Dragon by Paolo Uccello (c.1460)

😊 😃 EXPLORATION: Crusaders & Kings Game

At the end of this unit you'll find the Crusaders & Kings game board and game cards. The game board is divided into two halves. Print out both, match the halves together, and tape them into one board. Print the cards on to card stock or construction paper and cut them out. Each deck of cards should remain separate. To play, just draw a card from the stack that matches the path you're on and move as directed along your colored path. If you run out of cards, shuffle and start on the stack again. The first one to make it to the finish is the winner. Once you reach the finish though, you must draw a finish card and see what happens to you "after."

Before you start to play, set the scene:
You've been hearing rumors for years. The Holy City of Jerusalem was taken by the Muslims and now the word is that Christians living there are being enslaved and murdered. Worse, no one can travel to Jerusalem on pilgrimage. Many Christians need to make that journey; their souls are in peril if they can not absolve them with a journey to the relics at Jerusalem. There are other holy places and other relics, true, but the City of Jerusalem is the the most holy and the most potent of any city in the world. You've been thinking for awhile that something needed to be done about it. But the people in charge just seem to bicker and play politics. Last month a letter reached the Pope that the Emperor of Constantinople was asking for aid against the Turks who had been far too successful in taking land. The Byzantines were heretics, but they were better than the infidel Muslims. Then, just a week ago, Pope Urban gave a speech and asked kings and princes to gather

Additional Layer

Pope Gregory VII wanted to change the political status of the church and reform the clergy according to his idea of morality. These changes are known as Gregorian Reform. The church was transformed from being subject to kings to being an authority over them and independent of them. And the clergy were forced to take vows of celibacy.

Famous Folks

Peter the Hermit led 40,000 men and women on crusade in 1096. They were mostly indigent wards of the church and almost all of them died or were enslaved en route, but those who made it to Constantinople were a massive drain on resources while providing no real use.

Read more about Peter the Hermit and the People's Crusade.

CRUSADES – BALKANS – DIGESTIVE & SENSES – RELIGIOUS ART

Additional Layer

Krak des Chevaliers is a castle in Syria that was run and held by the Knights Hospitallers from 1142 to 1271. It is one of the best preserved medieval castles in the world.

Photo by Bernard Gagnon and shared under CC license.

You can see some amazing pictures of the castle here: http://www.historvius.com/krak-des-chevaliers-19/pictures/1300/

Additional Layer

Just War Doctrine gives the conditions under which war or violence can be resorted to morally.

The war must be the last resort; it must be done to protect innocent life; it must be done within a legitimate political authority. The popes of the 11th century decided the Crusades were a just war because of the need to protect pilgrims and Christians in the Holy Land.

What do you think? Is war ever justified? When?

their forces for an attack on the Holy Land. He described some of the things that had been done to Christian pilgrims and the tales turned your stomach. You've been unable to think of anything else since you heard the word. You decide to join.

If you want to join at Bruges with the Peasants' Crusade put your piece on the dark blue space with the number 1.

If you want to join at Clermont with the Prince's Crusade of Knights put your piece on the light blue space with the number 2.

Once you've chosen your path, follow the instructions on the cards as you play.

☺ ☺ EXPLORATION: So You Want to Go on Crusade?

Anyone and everyone who wanted to could go on crusade to the Holy Land. Below is a list of some of the people who might have gone. Choose which one you would want to be and research who they were, how they dressed, how they traveled to the Holy Land and how successful they were at war. Write a description or story about your travel to the Holy Land as that character.

- Knight Templar
- Knight Hospitaller
- Teutonic Knight
- Wealthy Baron
- King or Queen
- Nun or Priest
- Noble Lady
- Peasant man or woman
- Orphan Child
- Merchant

☺ ☺ ☺ EXPLORATION: Knights Hospitallers

The Knights Hospitallers were an order of militant Knights, but they didn't start out that way. Their original mission was to provide hospitality for pilgrims traveling to the Holy Land. They set up inns and hostels and provided food and medical care to European Christians traveling to and from Jerusalem from about 600 AD to 1099 AD when the First Crusade took place. From that point on, the order became half militaristic and half monastic, still fulfilling their mission to provide hospitality to travelers, but also recognizing that to do so they had

CRUSADES – BALKANS – DIGESTIVE & SENSES – RELIGIOUS ART

to be able to defend their territory with the sword. They became an official militant order in 1113 AD. Their uniform was a black surcoat with a white cross, worn over their armor. They became renowned for their prowess in the Crusades. Their base was the island of Rhodes in the Mediterranean. They spent the next couple hundred years fighting the Barbary Pirates, the sultan of Egypt, and the Ottoman sultan. Without the Knights Hospitallers no European trade could have happened in the Mediterranean and much of Europe would probably have become Muslim by conquest.

Make an army of Knights Hospitallers. Start with peggies, little wooden "people" you can buy at craft stores. Then paint them like a Knight Hospitaller. Paint the head flesh colored, the body black, a black helmet, gray chain mail hood and a white cross. Give him a face with a fine point Sharpie.

😊 🟢 ● EXPLORATION: The Siege of Rhodes

In 1480 the mighty Ottoman Empire, at the height of its power, attacked the little garrison of Knights Hospitallers on the Island of Rhodes. 80,000 Ottoman Turks in 160 ships faced less than 3,500 knights and soldiers in the city. 2,500 of these soldiers had

Additional Layer

From the 6th century and on, the most influential of the church movements were the Benedictine Monks. Each monastery was independent and operated with the goal of bringing the members closer to Christ. The Abbey at Cluny in France became the most important of the Benedictine monasteries.

Learn more about what it would have been like to live in an abbey or monastery as a monk or nun.

http://www.pluscardenabbey.org/home.asp

On the Web

Today medieval churches are stark gray stone, but when they were built they were brightly painted and inlaid with gold. Paint one yourself at

http://www.bbc.co.uk/history/british/middle_ages/launch_gms_paint_wells.shtml

Fabulous Fact

Rhodes was the ancient site of the Great Colossus, one of the wonders of the ancient world. The last bits of it had been carted off by earlier invading armies.

Crusades – Balkans – Digestive & Senses – Religious Art

Fabulous Fact
The Street of the Knights in Rhodes is one of the best preserved medieval locations on Earth. It looks just like it did in 1480 when the Turks were attacking.

Photo by Shadowgate and shared under CC license on Wikimedia.

On the Web
This video is about the siege of Rhodes http://youtu.be/9tMwvqlIw6A.

Fabulous Fact
Jews and women were banned from Richard the Lionheart's coronation ceremony. An untrue rumor spread that Richard was going to have all the Jews in London killed. Mass hysteria took over and many hundreds of Jews were killed, raped, and beaten, their property destroyed. Richard punished the worst of the perpetrators with death.

flown to the aid of the Hospitallers from Italy when the Turks first appeared.

The first target was the Tower of St. Nicholas, which commanded the harbor. The Turks fired upon the tower with their cannon for several days, then made an infantry assault. Grand Master Pierre d'Aubusson rushed personally to the defense of the walls, encouraging his men. The attack was repelled. Meanwhile, the knights and peasants inside the walls were busy shoring up the weakest point of the fortification on the eastern side of the tower by digging an internal moat and creating an additional wall. When the Turks attacked at this formerly weak point, the Hospitallers, suffering many casualties, fended off the Turks once again. Finally, the Turks attacked the Jewish quarter of the city and managed to get 2,500 Janissaries inside the walls, nearly as many as the knights were in total. After hours of bitter fighting with the head of the order, d'Aubusson leading the charges and wielding a lance while injured in five places, the Turks were expelled from the city. The standard of Islam was captured, and the Muslim soldiers fled in disorder. They wouldn't return for another forty years.

Siege of Rhodes 1480

The third attack was made on the Jewish Quarter in the city and nearly succeeded, but for the great valor of the knights.

Here is the tower of St. Nicholas, which the Turks attacked twice, being defeated with great losses on both sides.

Build city fortifications from cardboard and paper tubes and set up the defense of Rhodes. You can use the wooden people from the Knights Hospitallers Exploration to act out the battles.

CRUSADES – BALKANS – DIGESTIVE & SENSES – RELIGIOUS ART

😊 😊 😊 EXPLORATION: Richard the Lionheart

By the age of sixteen Richard I was already a war leader, a commander of men, and had put down rebellions against his father back in England. He was loved by his people, though he hardly knew them, speaking mostly French and spending almost all of his time on his estates in France, though he had been born in England. But they knew he was a soldier for Christ and brought great honor and renown to the crusader cause and to England as leader over all the Christian forces during the Third Crusade. In 1190 he left England with 8,000 soldiers and 100 ships. On the way to the Holy Land Richard was offended by the ruler of Cyprus, one Isaac Komnenos. Richard quickly took the island by force and appointed governors who sold it to the Knights Templar sometime later. The capture of this island kept the shipping lanes open for the Christian Crusaders.

Richard says farewell to the Holy Land

Once in the Holy Land, Richard quickly aided in the capture of the city of Acre. The leaders of the attack quarreled over the spoils and left Richard alone. He, unable to bring the 2,700 prisoners with him on campaign, put them to the sword. He then beat Saladin at the Battle of Arsuf in September of 1191. Before they had even taken the city, the crusaders held an election for the King of Jerusalem. Richard was not chosen and his opponent was killed by assassins four days before he could be crowned. The murder was never solved, but many suspect Richard. Richard continued to skirmish with Saladin, neither gaining the upper hand. Meanwhile, back home Richard was hearing rumors that his brother John was plotting against him as well as the French king Phillip. Richard had to go home or lose his kingdom.

Memorization Station

The Crusades were expensive, and lords and kings who went on them had to empty the nation's coffers, sell off lands and favors, and raise taxes to pay for the armies, supplies, and ships to get them to Jerusalem. This often caused great hardship to the poorest.

Sometimes they also borrowed money from local merchants. As surety, if the lord were unable to pay the debt the merchants would demand a charter of freedom for the town.

Famous Folks

Richard I married Berengaria of Navarre. It was a match promoted by Eleanor of Aquitaine, Richard's mother and one of the most powerful women of Europe.

The two women caught up with Richard while he was on his way to a crusade in the Holy Land. Richard and Berengaria were married. They spent very little time together though, as Richard was busy for the rest of his life fighting in campaign after campaign. He neglected his wife and they both died childless.

Crusades – Balkans – Digestive & Senses – Religious Art

Fabulous Fact
The rats that harbor the Bubonic plague have always been endemic to Southeast Asia. The Mongol invasions of the 14th century transported the Plague to Europe where the people had no resistance to the disease.

Additional Layer
One of the positive side effects of the plague was that it sparked curiosity among healers and scholars. They began to look at the real causes for diseases and how our bodies work. They began cutting up human corpses and learning about organs and body systems.

Can you think of another major tragedy that had some positive outcomes? How about in your personal life?

Fabulous Fact
During the times of the Plague criminals were released from jails because there were simply not enough people left to guard them.

On the way home he was shipwrecked and forced to proceed lengthwise through Central Europe. He traveled in disguise, but was recognized and captured by the Duke of Austria who accused Richard of having his cousin killed (Remember the assassins?). It was many, many weeks before the people of England knew what had happened to their king. When they did find out, they were dismayed. The Duke of Austria was demanding a huge ransom. The taxes would be enormous.

Richard finally made his way home, forgave John, named him his heir, and set about reconquering his troublesome French territories. In the end, Richard died from a crossbow bolt shot by a boy who defended a castle in Normandy which Richard was attempting to take.

Most people agree Richard was a stupendous soldier, and a brave and undaunted knight, but a terrible ruler and a not very nice person.

At the end of this unit you will find the triple lion coat of arms of King Richard in both color and in pencil sketch. Chose the one you like and paste it onto a cardboard shield.

☺☺☺ EXPLORATION: Bubonic Plague Symptoms
It started with a fever followed by red circles, which quickly became black and filled with pus until they were hard little balls, swelling and growing larger by the hour. Soon the patient was wracked with pain and delirious. In a couple of days they were dead. Very few survived. To stop the spread people burned the bodies, the clothes, the homes and everything else to do with the dead. They quarantined the sick, fled to the country, and prayed and repented in sackcloth. Too bad it didn't work. The Plague rushed on.

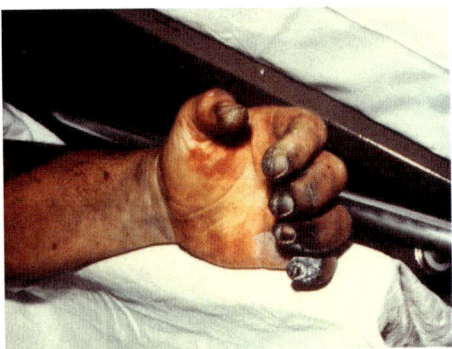

One of the symptoms of Bubonic Plague is that the fingers get gangrene and die, turning them black, hence, Black Death.

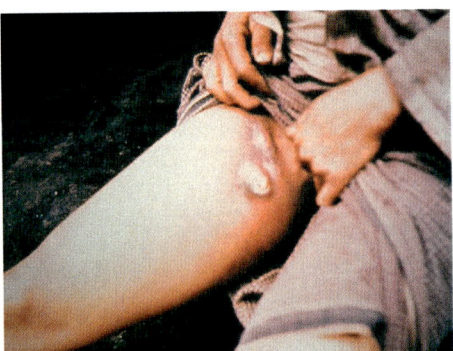

This patient has swollen and ruptured lymph nodes, called Buboes.

Crusades – Balkans – Digestive & Senses – Religious Art

To make the plague come alive, enlist the help of an assistant – maybe an older child or a spouse. Have them dress in medieval clothes, like a tunic and trousers with a belt . . . a little ragged wouldn't hurt. Put on makeup to simulate red circles and blackened skin. Add a few red spots to simulate flea bites. Lip pencil, mascara and blush work great. Place the sores where there are glands in the neck and under the arms. Flick a bit of water on the face to simulate a fever and darken the area under your eyes with a bit of mascara smeared around.

Begin to explain some aspect of the Middle Ages, such as cathedrals or monks or whatever you were working on last week. Just after you begin, your assistant staggers into the room and collapses, all while coughing violently. Pretend to be concerned and discover the symptoms of the Plague. Now get all excited! Finish up by explaining how the Plague is actually spread, through fleas which infect rats and then bite humans. Plague is a bacterial infection and with modern antibiotics can be cured, but back then it was almost always fatal.

☺ ☺ ☺ **EXPLORATION: The Spread of Bubonic Plague**
Use the Spread of the Bubonic Plague map from the end of this unit. Show the area of origin in east Asia, the route the Black Death took across Asia to Europe, and the spread across Europe. Write in the dates that the Black Death broke out in each area.

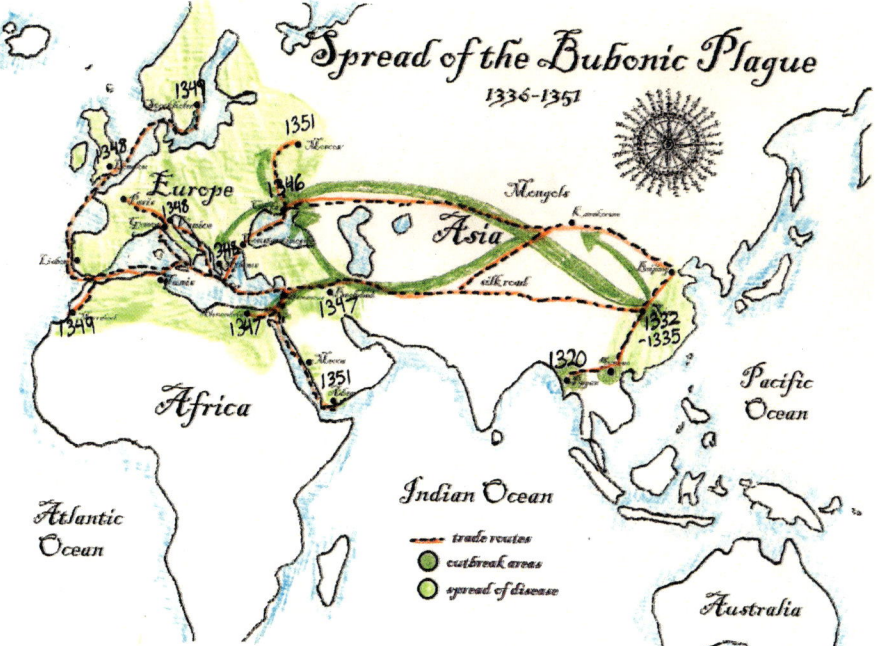

☺ ☺ ☺ **EXPLORATION: Spreading the Plague**
Bacterial illnesses like the Plague can be difficult to contain. Show how quickly germs and bacteria can be spread by putting

Additional Layer
Along with the coming of the Black Death, folk healers began selling all kinds of futile cures. Some recommended drinking urine. Others sold concoctions of things like ground up marigolds, eggshells, and treacle in alcohol. Some even suggested holding on to a live hen so the disease would be drawn out of their bodies and into the bird.

Before you laugh at them though, consider how ignorant we still are of many diseases and cures. In 100 years people will be amazed that we didn't even understand cancer.

Fabulous Fact
Many people of the time believed that the Plague was sent as a punishment from God for human sins. The church even held special services in an attempt to protect the people from God's wrath.

On the Web
Take this virtual tour of a medieval monastery.

http://youtu.be/hiPkLFGBK_U

Or watch these how-to in the Middle Ages videos:
http://www.english-heritage.org.uk/about/multimedia-library/how-to/

CRUSADES – BALKANS – DIGESTIVE & SENSES – RELIGIOUS ART

Additional Layer

Governments and medical organizations like the CDC (Centers for Disease Control) and the WHO (World Health Organization) are always worried about a major outbreak occurring. With the way the world is interconnected disease could spread very, very rapidly. And if it's something few people have immunity to, like smallpox, millions would be wiped out in a matter of months. Find out what governments do to watch for and try to prevent outbreaks.

lotion on to one person's hands, and then sprinkling them with glitter liberally. Now go about doing what you do – shake hands with others and interact. At some point stop and take a look at how much the glitter has spread and how many people it has affected. Compare this with the spread of bacterial disease. This is a great OUTDOOR activity if you don't want glitter all over the place inside.

Following the Black Death people became much more interested in disease and medicine. Girolama Fracas Toro, an Italian doctor, theorized that diseases could be spread long distances by invisible carriers (germs).

☺ ☺ ☺ **EXPLORATION: Population Decline**

During the time of the Plague about 1 in every 3 people died. Imagine if something like that were to happen in the U.S.A. Look up the current population and divide it by 3 to determine how many lives a similar plague would cost today.

Now look up and compare that with the number of U.S. lives lost in combat in each of these wars:

Revolutionary War	
Civil War	
World War I	
World War II	

Imagine the devastation.

☺ ☺ ☺ **EXPLORATION: Monks and Monasteries**

Monks who lived in monasteries lived lives of prayer, mediation, and a lot of hard work. Monasteries provided all kinds of services. They were places to stay for travelers; there were no hotels. They were a place for sick people to stay, rest, and be healed; there were no hospitals. They were also a place where books were made and stored; there were no publishing houses or libraries. Monks also gardened, made useful items, and provided goods for the monastery to sell to get money.

At a time with so much devastation in Europe, monks helped to keep hope and learning alive. Go visit this site and learn more about a medieval monastery:
http://www.cartage.org.lb/en/themes/GeogHist/histories/middleages/lifemiddle/1lisa.htm

Additional Layer

Monks helped keep learning alive by copying and preserving books at a time when much of Europe was too consumed with war and disease to worry about literature and art. The books monks copied and illuminated were works of art. They worked tirelessly in scriptoriums, rooms in the monastery set aside for the making of books. Those books are treasures from this dark time of Europe.

CRUSADES – BALKANS – DIGESTIVE & SENSES – RELIGIOUS ART

GEOGRAPHY: BALKANS

The Balkan states include Albania, Bosnia and Herzegovina, Bulgaria, Croatia, Greece, Kosovo, Montenegro, Serbia, and Macedonia. These are the countries on the Balkan Peninsula in Southeast Europe. These countries were anciently part of Byzantium, then fell under Muslim Turkish rule and were only freed with World War I. During the Cold War most of the region was under communist governments and under the control of the Soviet Union. They are still recovering economically from that period. They are also learning to govern themselves after centuries of autocratic rule. Today all of these countries are republics in various forms. They have market economies, but many lean heavily toward socialism, which has caused great financial crises.

Additional Layer
Kosovo is a disputed country. In February, 2008 Kosovo declared its independence, but Serbia still claims it as a territory. Kosovo has been recognized by 100 different countries including the U.K., France, and the U.S.A.

Fabulous Fact
Borders in the Balkans have shifted a lot in the last twenty years or so. If you have an atlas that is even a few years old, it may not be correct. In particular you may be missing the country of Kosovo.

Tsarevets, a medieval castle in Bulgaria

The Balkan Peninsula is highly mountainous. It is surrounded on three sides by water – the Black Sea in the east, the Mediterranean in the south, and the Adriatic Sea to the west. Overall, the climate is warm and mild with wet winters. In the more northern areas there are hot, dry summers and cold, snowy winters. The whole peninsula used to be heavily wooded for the most part, but many areas have been denuded of trees, and bushes and grasses grow instead. Most of the land is poor for farming. However, olives and grapes, which do not require rich

Additional Layer
King Boris III of Bulgaria saved the Jewish population of Bulgaria during WWII by resisting Hitler and defying his demands that the Bulgarian Jews be deported in spite of Bulgaria's being an ally of Germany at this time. The people of Bulgaria also supported and defended their Jewish population. After Bulgaria became communist, virtually the entire population of Jews emigrated to Israel.

CRUSADES – BALKANS – DIGESTIVE & SENSES – RELIGIOUS ART

Additional Layer
Burek is a Bosnian meat pie, formed into a snail shape.

Photo by Nikola Škorić

Roll this filling:

1 ½ lbs. ground beef
3 diced onions
2 beaten eggs
2 Tbsp. paprika
Salt & pepper to taste
½ cup melted butter

into premade filo dough. Then place the roll in the center of a baking sheet and form into a snail shape. Bake at 375° F for 35-40 minutes.

Famous Folks
Nikola Tesla was a Serbian. He moved to America in 1884. He invented x-ray technology, radio, AC current, and about 300 other things.

soil and do well in the dry heat, grow well in this region. There are very few deposits of either petroleum or minerals.

The majority of the people in the Balkans are Orthodox Christians (Greek Church), the rest are Roman Catholic or Muslim. There are some small, ancient Jewish communities in the region as well. Most of the Jews were killed or fled during the Holocaust of World War II.

The Balkans are at a crossroads between Asia and Europe and have been the home of many dozens of ethnic groups. Dozens of languages are spoken through the area in the Hellenic, Albanian, Turkic, Latin, and Slavic language groups.

Most people in the Balkans live in cities. Athens, Belgrade, Bucharest, and Sofia each have populations of more than one million.

Downtown Sofia, Bulgaria. Photo by Boby Dimitrov, CC license.

☺ ☺ ● EXPLORATION: Danube Adventure
Travel down the Danube River from the northern border of Serbia to the Black Sea. Imagine you are taking a river boat ride downriver. What do you see along the way? Which cities do you stop in? Which countries do you pass through? Make a poster, with a large map of the river and pictures posted along the way. Write captions telling what you see and do.

CRUSADES – BALKANS – DIGESTIVE & SENSES – RELIGIOUS ART

☺ ☺ ☺ **EXPLORATION: Balkan States Map**

Color a map of the Balkan states. You can find an outline map at the end of this unit. Use an atlas to label each country and capital city, the major surrounding bodies of water, the major rivers, and the Balkan Mountains.

☺ ☺ ☺ **EXPLORATION: Travel Brochure**

Create a travel brochure for one of the Balkan countries. Find out what natural attractions and cities are tourist friendly. Draw pictures and write captions. Tell where the principle airport is located and describe the wonderful hotel and a famous local dish. You will find a Travel Brochure template to print at the end of this unit.

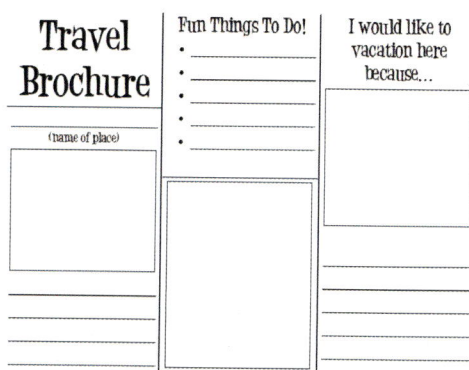

Additional Layer

Montenegro became independent of Serbia in 2006 by a vote which was overseen by the European Union.

On the Web

The oro is a traditional (and very energetic) dance from Montenegro. At the end of the dance the men jump on each others' shoulders to dance.

http://youtu.be/O8LXrsrwE7Y

According to the description on the video the whole thing is done to impress the girls. Seems about right.

Additional Layer

Feta cheese is a traditional Greek variety and eaten all over the Balkans. It is made primarily from sheep's milk. Get some from the grocery store and try it.

Crusades – Balkans – Digestive & Senses – Religious Art

Additional Layer

The modern necktie descends from Croatia. Croatian soldiers were hired to fight for the King of France and Cardinal Richelieu in internal French intrigues. Their stylish neck cloths drew the attention of the French who began to copy the style. Eventually the cravat (a French corruption of "Croat") would morph into the necktie, a completely useless strip of cloth that men tie around their necks like nooses.

For Grown-ups Only

We try to keep recipes we use in these geography lessons very kid friendly, but I couldn't pass up featuring this Greek spanakopita (Spinach Pie) and this very yummy Greek cook's blog.
http://mylittleexpatkitchen.blogspot.nl/2012/07/spanakopita.html

Writer's Workshop

Often the stories we write are about people, but it's really fun to write from an animal's point of view too. Choose an Albanian animal and create a story told from the animal's point of view.

☺ ☺ ☺ EXPEDITION: Book It!

Visit a travel agency. Arrange ahead of time to visit a travel agency and have them assist your child in coming up with a travel itinerary to one of these countries. Calculate the hypothetical costs and see if you can get some travel brochures of the area. Display the information in your notebook.

☺ ☺ EXPLORATION: Puzzle Map

Make a puzzle out of the map of the Balkan States. Glue it to cardboard or poster board to make it more durable. If you make separate tags with the labels of each country you can practice putting the puzzle together and naming each of the countries.

☺ ☺ ☺ EXPLORATION: Choose Your Own Book Project

Choose one of the story books from the library list and make a book project about it. Include scenes from the book and a little background information about the country.

☺ ☺ EXPLORATION: Country Poster

Choose one of the Balkan countries and make a poster about it. You might include a map, flag, fun facts, and sections on holidays, culture, clothing, and other interesting things you find out.

☺ ☺ EXPLORATION: Albanian Animals

Albania is richly forested and mountainous. There is great diversity of wildlife including brown bear, gray wolf, chamois, vultures, wild boar, lynx, pine marten, and other wild cats. The Golden Eagle, the symbol of Albania is also found there.

Golden eagles are endemic to most of the northern hemisphere, Europe, Asia, and North America. They don't do well in places where human populations rise. They are birds of prey and swoop down to catch mice, rabbits, snakes, marmots, foxes, and other small animals including baby deer, sheep, and goats. If prey is scarce they will also eat carrion, dead animals, and they can take on bigger animals like

CRUSADES – BALKANS – DIGESTIVE & SENSES – RELIGIOUS ART

swans, canines, and cranes. Golden Eagles have been used by people in falconry for thousands of years to hunt dangerous and larger prey such as wolves. Many cultures around the world reverence the powerful and noble birds. They mate for life and nest in tall tress or on the sides of cliffs.

Make the Golden Eagle Craft from the end of this unit. Start by printing the eagle shape onto brown construction paper or card stock (or you can color it in on white paper if you like). Add feathers on as desired. Then attach the whole eagle to a toilet paper tube. Inside the toilet paper tube on the side closest to the eagle, attach a straw. Thread a string through the straw. Now your kids, one holding each end, can make the eagle fly back and forth between them.

😊 🟢 EXPLORATION: Bulgarian Martenitsa

Bulgarians wear the little martenitsa doll on their wrist or pinned to their clothes all through the month of Baba Marta, Grandmother March. March is the beginning of spring in Bulgarian folklore and must be welcomed in, sending winter on its way. The martenitsa dolls are always made of white and red yarn. The red symbolizes life and passion while white symbolizes purity. The two together symbolize a wish for good health.

Make your own martenitsa doll. You'll need red and white yarn, a form to wrap the yarn around (a book or cardboard) and scissors.

1. Wrap a length of yarn around and around a form. I used a book. You could use a piece of cardboard or any other similar object. The book I used was about 5" across. The larger the form, the larger your doll will turn out. The exact size doesn't matter.
2. Remove the yarn loop from

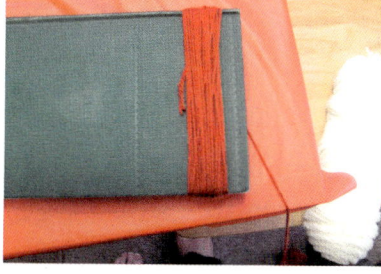

Fabulous Fact
The name Montenegro means Black Mountain. The name dates back to the Middle Ages and comes from the name of a noble ruling family.

Additional Layer
This is an Orthodox church in Macedonia.

Most people in this region belong to the Orthodox religion.

The architecture style is very typical of Orthodox churches. They are compact and the central dome represents the heavens. From the center there are square extensions at each of the four points of the compass, forming a cross shape.

Inside the church the altar is always at the eastern end. Traditionally there are no pews for church goers, everybody stands because it was considered disrespectful to sit during the ceremony. Learn more about the Orthodox religion and Orthodox church buildings.

CRUSADES – BALKANS – DIGESTIVE & SENSES – RELIGIOUS ART

Additional Layer

Macedonia borders the region of Greece which is also called Macedonia. Greece is all mad because they think Macedonia should not call themselves Macedonia since there could be confusion about which region is being referred to. Besides, the Greeks say, Macedonia is a Greek word and refers to Greek people, but you are Slavs. The Macedonians retaliated by building statues of Alexander the Great all over their country.

The two countries have taken it so far as to bring each other up before NATO and UN courts.

I actually think it's funny.

Famous Folks

Aristotle Onassis was a famous and fabulously wealthy Greek shipping magnate. Most of his wealth was obtained illegally by smuggling and fraudulent business practices. He married widow Jacqueline Kennedy in 1968.

the form. Tie it in about the middle with an alternating color (red if you started with white, white if you started with red).
3. Now you need to make another loop of yarn in white if you did the first in red or vice versa. This loop should be smaller by a couple of inches than the first. It will become the "arms" of your doll.
4. Remove the second loop from the form and insert it in the middle of the first loop above the spot where you tied it. Tie the first loop above the arms so the arms are snugged in nice and tight. This also makes the head.
5. Finally, tie the wrists of the doll and the ankles if you want a boy, or leave the skirt loose for a girl. Tie a loop of yarn on to the top. When spring really arrives hang it from a tree or bush just beginning to bud.

☺ ☺ ☻ **EXPLORATION: Greek Dance**

Greece is one of the few places in the world where people still perform their traditional dances not for tourists or to "preserve their culture" but as a normal part of their everyday lives. The dances are performed at weddings, family celebrations, and on holidays.

Each region or town has its own style of dancing.

Here is a Greek dance from central Greece:
http://youtu.be/hDoitkaU27I

Watch this you tube video and learn a basic Greek dance step:
http://youtu.be/EtKfru3fEWc

CRUSADES – BALKANS – DIGESTIVE & SENSES – RELIGIOUS ART

🙂 🙂 **EXPLORATION: Serbian Epic**
Epic poetry (think Beowulf, The Song of Roland, or the Epic of Gilgamesh) is sort of the national language of Serbia. It's in their blood. Even today people write epics and release them to the public domain. Other authors add to them or adjust and rework them just as ancient poets would have done. Serbian wiseguys create parody songs in epic style (but humorous) and release them on You Tube to great acclaim. Unfortunately, unless you speak Serbian you're probably not going to get the joke. Serbian politicians also stand on the steps of parliament and tell of the day's business in epic poetry . . . *I know, great idea, that would keep congress busy. "Before you can vote on that bill, it needs to be written as an epic poem." Keep 'em out of our hair, right? I think I'll propose a new amendment . . .*

Anyway, this site has a good, brief explanation of Serbian epic poetry, what it is and what it is not, along with some English translations. Most of the excerpts and poems are not too long, so enjoy!
http://home.earthlink.net/~markdlew/SerbEpic/index.htm

🙂 🙂 🙂 **EXPLORATION: Pogaca Bread**
This traditional yeasted flat bread is common in most of the Balkan states. Dip it in soup, stew, or Greek yogurt dip.

In a large bowl, mix and let rest five minutes:
    2 cups warm water
    2 tsp. yeast

Then add:
    1 ½ tsp. salt
    ¼ cup olive oil or melted butter
    7-8 cups flour, mixing in a little at a time, then kneading in the rest until it is no longer sticky.

Divide into three even parts and shape into rounds. Place on a greased baking sheet. Let rest for 20 minutes. Brush with beaten egg and poke the surface all over with a fork. Bake at 425°F for 25 minutes.

Additional Layer

The Gusle is an instrument unique to Serbia and is usually used to accompany a person reciting or singing an epic poem. Learn more about this instrument.

Additional Layer

This painting depicts a scene from the Battle of Kosovo as told in Serbian epic poetry.

Kosovo Maiden by Uros Predic, 1919

A lot of people have begun, boringly, to call this region "Southeast Europe" because the word "Balkans" has come to have negative, though not undeserved, connotations.

CRUSADES – BALKANS – DIGESTIVE & SENSES – RELIGIOUS ART

SCIENCE: DIGESTIVE SYSTEM & SENSES

Memorization Station
Memorize this little ditty:

The esophagus squeezes the food all down,
And into the stomach that's where it's found.
Gastric juices break down the food.
Stomach muscles churn so it's used.
Chew it up and swallow...
those itty bitty pieces...
Take out all the good stuff...
Turn it into feces.
Churn it up and swallow...
Turn it into goo...
Now we're singin' the digestion blues.
The pancreas and liver add insulin and bile.
It's only in them for a little while.
The gooey muck is like a line;
Its nutrients are now in the small intestine.
Chew it up and swallow...
those itty bitty pieces...
Take out all the good stuff...
Turn it into feces.
Churn it up and swallow....
Turn it into goo...
Now we're singin' the digestion blues.

Fabulous Fact
How long does it take your dinner to, well, exit the system? It depends on you. Food leaves your stomach after about two hours. It's probably another two hours until your small intestine is empty. But your large intestine can take anywhere from 12 to 50 hours to do its job.

Digestive System

Your digestive system is like a tube inside your body that begins at one end and runs clear to the other without ever actually entering your body. The rest of your body is protected from all that stuff you bring in by walls and mucous lining the organs. Digestion includes mechanical processes like chewing and churning, and also chemical processes like acids and enzymes.

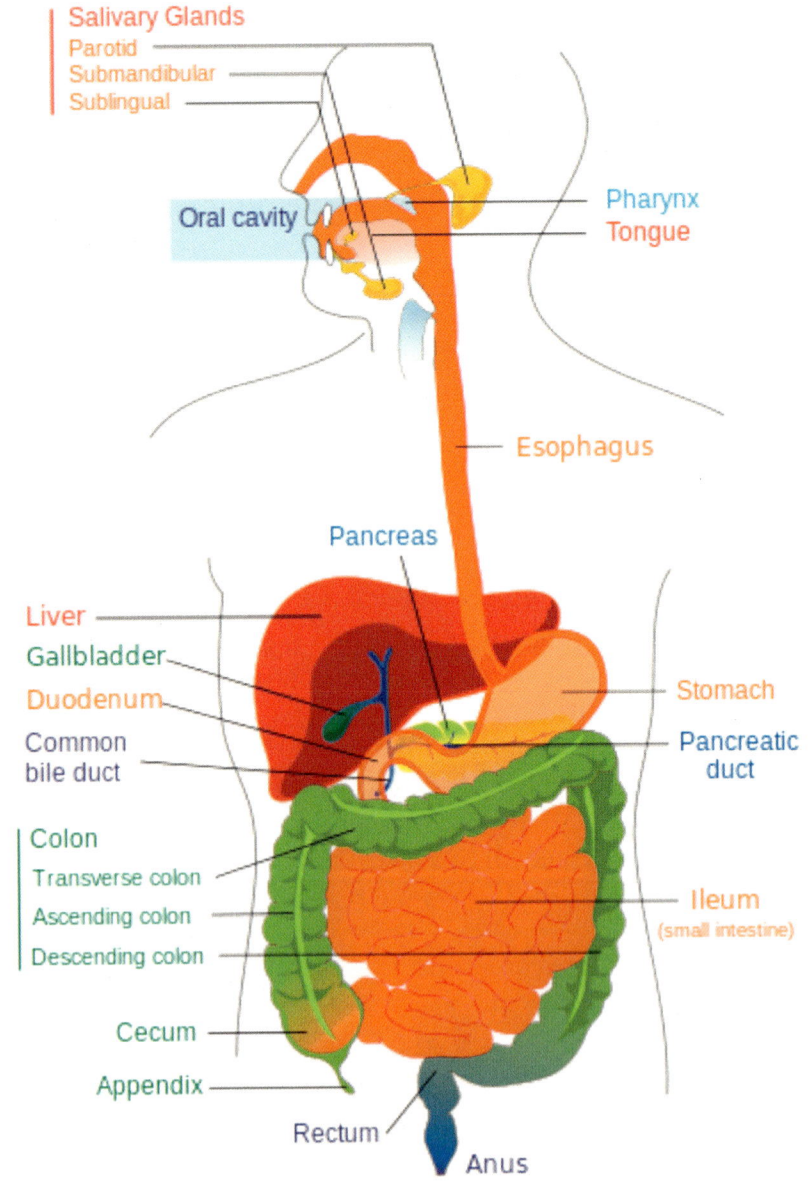

CRUSADES – BALKANS – DIGESTIVE & SENSES – RELIGIOUS ART

Senses
In order to react and act in your environment you need physical senses to help you. Humans have sight, hearing, pain sensations, pressure sensations, gravity sensors, balance, taste, and smell to help us get through this world. None of our senses are number one among animals in this world, but they are all pretty good.

☺ ☺ ☺ **EXPLORATION: Digestive System Body Picture**
Add the digestive system to the body picture you've still got hanging on that wall. Include the mouth, esophagus, stomach, small intestine, large intestine, gall bladder, pancreas, and liver. Use construction paper to make each of these parts. Then tape or glue them into place.

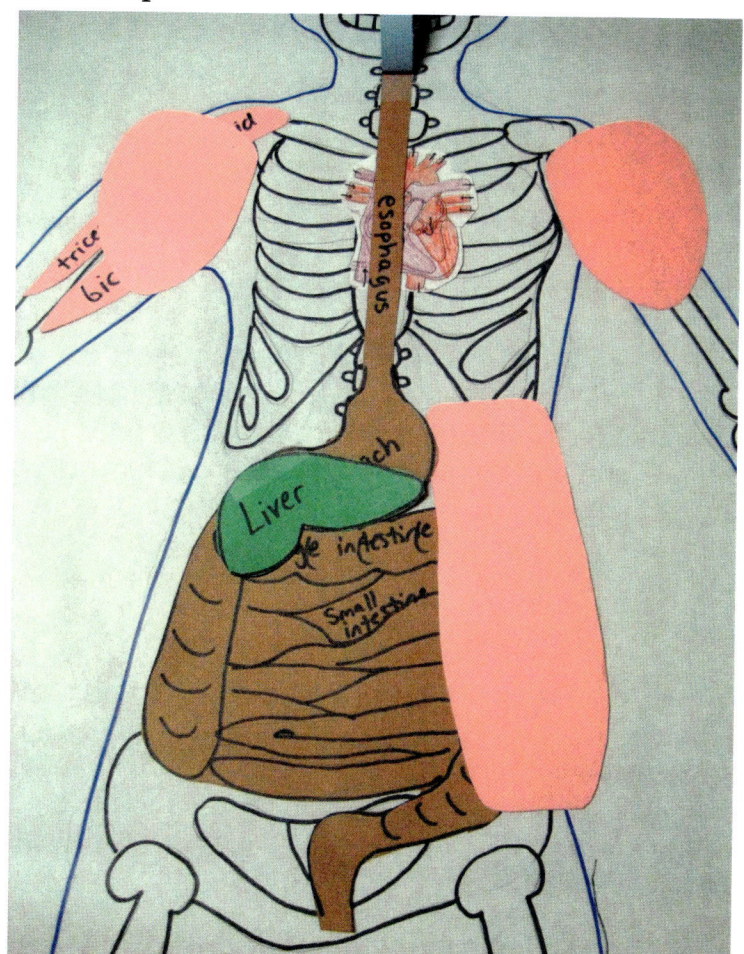

As you add each organ, read about its functions and rehearse what the job of each one is. Are there any we can live without?

☺ ☺ ☺ **EXPERIMENT: Digestion Starts in the Mouth**
Your mouth is the first means of digestion. First, you have teeth to chew up big chunks of food into smaller ones. Second, the saliva in your mouth begins the chemical breakup of food as well.

Additional Layer
Your digestive system is an important part of your immune system. The acidic environment of your stomach kills most bacteria and viruses that you swallow. Then the mucus lining the whole system also kills undesirables. There are certain enzymes that kill microorganisms and finally, the healthy normal bacteria in your system out competes anything that has survived the rest of it. Given all the muck we eat accidentally it's astonishing that we make it at all, but hardly anyone gets sick from normal bacteria ingested on a daily basis.

Additional Layer
The immune system is one of the body's most important features. Pick up a book or two on the topic to round out your study of the human body. The way we fight of disease is amazing.

On the Web
This National Geographic video of the digestive system uses an actual camera inside a body.
http://youtu.be/e3O1AdlC8bI
Preview first for gross-out factor.

CRUSADES – BALKANS – DIGESTIVE & SENSES – RELIGIOUS ART

On the Web
Mr. Anderson teaches about the digestive system.
http://youtu.be/nM5kMSjBrmw

Have your teen just browse through and watch all of Mr. Anderson's videos on biology. They are all excellent, teaching basically everything you would get from a standard high school course.

Additional Layer
There is an entire diet industry in the United States that is devoted to spreading information about food and nutrition. Many of the so-called "experts" disagree on the best path to health though. Many of them promise an easy, almost magical solution to health. Why do you think they make such claims? Is the information they share always accurate? How can you know what is true and best for your body?

On the Web
Watch this fun song about the five senses for little kids.
http://youtu.be/z7pi9kv1djo

1. Chew a soda cracker 25 times and spit the chewed bit out onto a napkin.
2. Place a whole undamaged cracker next to it.
3. Test the two crackers for starch content by dropping a bit of iodine onto each one.
4. In the presence of starch the dark brown iodine turns black. Has the chewed cracker changed?

☺ ☺ ☺ **EXPLORATION: Breaking It Down**
Our bodies break down our food into usable bits through our digestive system. As you talk about each process, demonstrate it using Rainbow Chips Deluxe Cookies. Start by putting the cookie in a baggie. As you crush it, talk about how our teeth break the food into small pieces. Add a little water and discuss the job saliva does in breaking the food down further. Next, begin squeezing and squishing the bag while describing the stomach's role in digestion. Now put a small sponge in the baggie and absorb the liquid out as you talk about our small intestine and our bodies absorbing nutrients through the blood stream. The remainder will be a brown mush; describe how our body gets rid of the waste at the end by traveling to the large intestine and then discarding the leftovers as feces.

☺ ☺ **EXPLORATION: You Are What You Eat**
Along with digestion, this is a great time to talk about health and what we should be feeding our bodies. Discuss what is healthful and the kinds of foods we should avoid. You can refer to the Food Pyramid. Then have each kid draw a picture of themselves made up of healthy foods. For example, a milk carton might be the body, a tomato for the head, green bean hair, arms and legs made of whole grain bread, and a carrot nose.

☺ ☺ **EXPLORATION: Simple Versus Complex**
Humans have complex digestive systems that take our food through a nutrient extracting process, and then discard the waste. Some animals have simpler digestive systems and some are even more complex than ours. The animal's needs determine it's digestive tract. Choose one of these animals to research and write a report about their digestion: owls, cows, flatworms, sea anemones.

☺ **EXPLORATION: Our World**
We learn about our world and everything in it by using our senses of sight, hearing, touch, taste, and smell. Discuss which of our organs are used for each of these senses. Now go somewhere out of your ordinary (maybe a park, a city bench, a shopping mall) and have the kids fill in these blanks descriptively in their writer's

CRUSADES – BALKANS – DIGESTIVE & SENSES – RELIGIOUS ART

notebooks:

My _____ see _____.
My _____ hear _____.
My _____ touches _____.
My _____ smells _____.
My _____ tastes _____.

Sketch the setting in your notebook as well.

☺ ☺ ☺ EXPLORATION: No Sense At All
What if you didn't have senses? Set up an obstacle course to show how much more difficult things would be without our senses.

In the first part, blindfold the kids and make them navigate through furniture that has been pulled into their way.

In the second part, put ear plugs in their ears and speaking in a normal volume give them the instructions on where they must go next.

In the third part, put oven mitts on their hands and make them pick a particular object out of a bag of objects and tell you what it is (make sure they can't see what they are doing either).

In the fourth section, have the kids spin until they are dizzy and then have them walk a board placed on the ground (or along a straight line).

In the fifth section, put nose plugs on and eat several types of fruit or several types of crackers (the textures should be similar) while blindfolded and identify what they have eaten.

When you finish, discuss how important our senses are to us and how we rely on them without even thinking about it.

☺ ☺ ☺ EXPLORATION: Diagram of the Eye
Color and label the diagram of the eye. You can find a printable diagram at the end of this unit

1. Optic Nerve
2. Retina
3. Lens
4. Cornea
5. Pupil
6. Iris
7. Vitreous Fluid

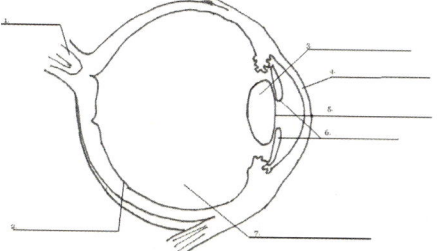

Additional Layer
Talk with someone who is blind, hearing impaired, or has another disability having to do with impairment of the senses.

How do they compensate?

What changes have they made in their lives to overcome this challenge?

Ask questions and find out more.

On the Web
Watch this most excellent ancient video on the eye. Your grandmother probably watched it in science class, but it's still very good.
http://youtu.be/sQRwViFoEBw

And here's one on the ear:
http://youtu.be/oDwUXAPQ_8U

Additional Layer
Animals and insects use smells to send messages to each other. Mostly, they put off smells to warn others to stay away. Cats, dogs, ladybugs, and even monarch butterflies put off scents to communicate messages.

Crusades – Balkans – Digestive & Senses – Religious Art

Famous Folks

Helen Keller became very sick at age two and ended up both blind and deaf from the illness. Read about her story, her struggles, and how much she overcame in the book *The Story of My Life* by Helen Keller.

Helen Keller, age 8, with her tutor Anne Sullivan.

Additional Layer

Why do things that just aren't true make it into books to be repeated over and over? Because the people who write the books probably just repeated what they found in another book and then people copied them and pretty soon you have a whole lot of authors agreeing on a complete myth. It actually happens a lot (probably in these books too, we're not perfect).

😊 😊 **EXPERIMENT: Dissect a Cow Eyeball**

You can get a preserved one from a science supply store, along with directions on how to dissect it and what to look for.

😊 😊 😊 **EXPERIMENT: Are You Left Eyed?**

You have a dominant eye, just like you have a dominant hand. You are either left-handed or right-handed. And you are either left-eyed or right-eyed. To find out which is your dominant eye, form your fingers into a triangle with your thumbs and pointer fingers overlapping each other. Stretch your hands out in front of you and pick a target at least ten feet away. Sight the target through the triangle of your fingers. Now close one eye and then the other without moving your hands. With one eye you will still see the target perfectly. This is your dominant eye. With the other eye, the target will disappear from the triangle of your fingers.

😊 😊 **EXPLORATION: Use Your Ears**

Use your sense of hearing in this game. An adult hides with a whistle. Then the adult blows the whistle repeatedly until the kids find the hider. Repeat with different people being the hider. Explain how you use your sense of hearing to find the hider.

Then watch this video for more information:
http://youtu.be/ahCbGjasm_E

😊 😊 😊 **EXPLORATION: What Can You Smell?**

Douse cotton balls in several different scents. Then have the kids try to identify what they are smelling. Here are some ideas: vanilla extract, rubbing alcohol, nail polish remover, mint extract, vinegar, pickle juice, perfume, hairspray, and anything else liquid. Use this as an introduction to talking about the sense of smell or learning about the structure of the nose.

😊 😊 😊 **EXPERIMENT: Make a Tongue Map of Myth**

In most text books tongue maps are shown depicting different parts of the tongue that can taste exclusively one basic taste. The reality is that every part of your tongue can taste every basic taste, but some parts may be more sensitive to certain tastes than

CRUSADES – BALKANS – DIGESTIVE & SENSES – RELIGIOUS ART

others. So we're going to try the tongue mapping thing anyway. Consider it original research into your tongue.

Draw a tongue shape on a piece of paper. Now use a cotton swab to dip into different substances to see which parts of your tongue can taste different things most predominantly. The basic things you can taste are sweet, salty, bitter, and sour. You can dip into sugar, salt, cocoa powder, and lemon juice. Now touch the sugar to the tip of your tongue. Can you taste it? Touch it to the sides, center, and so on. Where can you taste sweet? Mark it on your tongue map. Now repeat with the other tastes. Your tongue map may be unique to you, it may not look like everyone else's. Maybe you can taste salty all over, show that on your map.

☺ ☺ ☺ **EXPLORATION: Smell-a-licious Survey**
Take a survey of your friends' favorite smells and tastes. Display the results on a graph to see which are the most popular. Now create a Venn diagram of the data. Is there an overlap between favorite tastes and smells?

☺ ☺ ☺ **EXPLORATION: Memories**
The things we like the smell and taste of are often memory-responses. For example, I love the smell of fresh, cut grass because I have many happy memories of playing outside on Saturday mornings while my dad trimmed the lawn. On the other hand, I can't eat mushrooms to this day because of a science lesson I had about the formation of fungus in junior high. Can you think of any taste/smell memories you have that have shaped your opinions? Write about them.

☺ ☺ ☺ **EXPLORATION: My Food's Path**
Start by naming your favorite food. Now trace its path as you eat it. Which of your senses get used? Describe it using your senses. Now trace its path through digestion. What happens in your mouth? In your stomach? In your intestines? What other parts of your body benefit from the specific nutrients and vitamins it provides? Is your gall bladder involved? How about your liver? Follow the food along its routes and discuss what processes are happening and how the food benefits your body.

Umami

So there are five basic tastes:

Sweet

Salty

Bitter

Sour

and Umami

Umami is a savory flavor found frequently in Asian cuisine. The word is in fact Japanese, since in the west there is no word for this flavor, being rather short on soy sauce in former days.

You can taste the flavor in cheese and in soy sauce. Eat some and pay attention to the tastes. Can you taste umami?

There might very well be other basic tastes no one has bothered to name and identify. The way we taste things is one of the least researched bits about the human body.

Fabulous Fact

But, you protest, I can taste lots of other things besides salty, sweet, bitter, sour and that umami thingy. Yes, but almost all the rest of tasting is actually smell. Try tasting a strawberry with your nose plugged. Not quite the same is it?

CRUSADES – BALKANS – DIGESTIVE & SENSES – RELIGIOUS ART

THE ARTS: RELIGIOUS ART

Additional Layer

Gothic art started with stone. Buildings and sculpture created for those buildings were the first expression of the Gothic style. It was a hundred years later that frescoes and paintings in the Gothic style began to appear.

Additional Layer

Today when people talk about "gothic" or "goth" they usually mean dark, black, heavy, depressing, sometimes with an overtone of magic. People who dress goth wear dark clothes and heavy eye make-up. This has nothing whatsoever to do with the Gothic art period.

Additional Layer

Sculptures and paintings depicting Mary cradling the dead body of Jesus are called Pietà and are an important subject for medieval art.

During the Gothic Period most of the art was religious. It was the church that had the money and the monks that had the leisure to commission art and create non-essential-for-life stuff. In addition, spiritual life was central to everyday life for the average medieval person. Prayers, saints' days, and the authority of the church occupied normal life. Scenes from the Bible adorned the walls and ceilings of buildings. Art was mostly intended to be inspirational and paintings were filled with symbolism and spiritual themes.

Virgin of Mercy with St. John and St. Mary Magdalene, called Pieta Récollets. This little stauette is in the Church of Recollets in Toulous, France. It was created sometime in the 16th century by an unknown artist.

Besides the artists who were either amateurs or commissioned for their work, monks also created a lot of art. Monks in monasteries often served as scribes and also painted, creating beautiful and inspiring pieces.

🙂 🟢 🔵 **EXPLORATION: Silver Leaf**
Gold and silver leafing was common among Gothic art. The artist applied metallic touches to parts of the painting that they wanted to stand out or glow. For example, if an angel was painted, it may be surrounded by gold leaf to signify its closeness to deity.

Fra (meaning Brother) Angelico de Fiesoie was an Italian monk and a brilliant painter. He learned to paint while living in the monastery and covered its walls with scenes from the Bible. He

CRUSADES – BALKANS – DIGESTIVE & SENSES – RELIGIOUS ART

then added bits of gold pieces to the scenes to make them shimmer. The people he painted that were righteous were usually adorned with golden halos to represent their goodness. He didn't just use gold paints though; he actually put metal on the walls.

Additional Layer
The Rainbow Fish by Marcus Pfister is a perfect example of this combination of paint and metal in a modern format.

This is an altarpiece painted by Fra Angelico in about 1437. Notice the amount of gold. An altarpiece would have been suspended from the wall behind the altar in a church.

Sketch a picture on a sheet of construction paper. It could be a crown with jewels, a robot, a space ship, or even a scene from the Bible. Paint the picture and then incorporate bits of foil that are glued on in the areas you want to accentuate.

😊 😊 😊 EXPLORATION: Gold Leafing
Gold leafing an entire picture is really easy. Just take a photo to a copy center and have them make a color copy on a clear transparency sheet. Put an even coat of spray adhesive on the back side of the transparency, then stick thin, delicately crumpled sheets of gold leaf on to it, being careful not to miss any spots.

Gold leafing can be purchased at most craft stores. It comes in a booklet with really thin sheets. You just wrinkle the sheet a little, then stick it right on to the transparency. Fill in little holes with more sheets of gold leaf as necessary. It looks most beautiful if you frame it to hide the unfinished edges.

Additional Layer
Is religion a prevalent part of our modern world? Can you look around your house and town and find religious references? In some ways it seems that religion is becoming less and less a part of our society, but America was most certainly founded on religious principles. Look at our money; even our currency testifies of common beliefs of early Americans.

Our law system and our belief in the value of the individual are also based on Christian philosophy.

CRUSADES – BALKANS – DIGESTIVE & SENSES – RELIGIOUS ART

Additional Layer

Commissioning art is not just a thing of the past, and competing for the job isn't either. Often when a city or company wants to include an art installation they will ask artists to submit their plans and ideas. The plans are reviewed and a winning artist is selected to take on the job.

My son has an art gallery on his bedroom wall and sells me his work to make money. I often request specific pieces for my fridge, especially to accompany upcoming holidays. My spare change is worth the amount of time he spends in his sketchbook. Art and entrepreneurship, gotta love that.

Additional Layer

Typically information is transmitted over generations through the written word, but in medieval times there were many stories, poems, and songs that were memorized and passed down orally, even impossibly long ones. Memorization was an art, but the written word is still more reliable.

Be careful not to get adhesive on your fingertips before you touch the gold leafing because it will stick to your fingers instead of the picture.

😊 😊 😊 EXPLORATION: And the Winner Is . . .

In Florence, Italy there was a small church, but its poor doors needed decorating. The city held a competition to decide which artist should be hired for the job. Lorenzo Ghiberti won the honor. He was not only an artist, but also a goldsmith, and the judges were smitten by the gold he added into his paintings. He spent twenty years of his life working on those doors!

These are the doors on the north side of the Baptistry, known as the "Gates of Paradise"

You can create a scene in a similar style to the way he made the doors. Start with a piece of cardboard, like from a box. Draw a design using glue and then adhere yarn to the design. Lay a piece of heavy foil over the top and press it down on the design until you can clearly see the picture. Paint it all black and let it dry really well. You can use steel wool to gently rub the paint off all of the high spots, leaving the low spots dark. That's a relief!

😊 😊 😊 EXPLORATION: Copy Book

Monks spent much of their lives copying scriptures, prayers, and psalms. One monk said, "Every word you write is a blow that smites the devil." Copy down a scripture word for word, and then turn it into a piece of art in your own style.

😊 😊 😊 EXPLORATION: Workshops

Artists were viewed as craftsmen just like weavers, smiths, or masons. They usually worked in workshops collectively, so one painter was often not the only one to work on a piece. This is one reason why there is a lot of debate over which works should be credited to which artists during this era. Often the workshop was commissioned to make a specific piece, and the group of painters would all spend a year or so on it before they were done.

CRUSADES – BALKANS – DIGESTIVE & SENSES – RELIGIOUS ART

Hang a large sheet of butcher paper on the wall. Get out the paints and brushes and have everyone collaborate together on one painting.

😊 😊 😊 EXPLORATION: The Wilton Diptych

The Wilton Diptych is a painting of King Richard kneeling in front of Jesus, the Virgin Mary, and angels. No one knows for sure who painted it, but it's known as the Wilton diptych because it was kept in the Wilton House. It is thought to have originally belonged to King Richard himself. The painting was done on a diptych. A diptych is a set of two panels, connected together by hinges. It can be carried around, folded up, or set on its own to stand up on an altar. Other artists also painted triptychs, three paneled paintings.

Make your own diptych or triptych by cutting several panels out of wood and then connecting them with hinges. If you don't have a suitable saw, most home improvement stores will do straight cuts for you. Paint a picture on your diptych. Even though you are using two or three panels, you should consider it one painting. All of the panels were parts of the same picture.

> **Additional Layer**
> Wilton House is a manor in the English countryside. It was once an abbey. When Henry VIII dissolved all the abbeys he turned it over to the Earl of Pembroke, William Herbert, who was a favorite of the king.
>
>
>
> *Wilton House, shared by John Goodall, CC license*

😊 😊 😊 EXPLORATION: I Spy
Look through an art book at Gothic paintings. Search for some of these symbols:
- Keys (represent St. Peter, keeper of the keys to heaven)
- Dove (represents the holy spirit)
- Palm leaf (represents a martyr who died for their belief in

> **Additional Layer**
> If you look closely you can see several small white deer on the Wilton Diptych. That was King Richard's symbol. Also, notice how the earthly ground is plain, but the heavenly ground is adorned with flowers. The picture intends to send the message that King Richard's reign was favored by God himself. The painting is full of symbolism. You can read more about it by searching the Wikipedia article entitled The Wilton Diptych.
> http://www.nationalgallery.org.uk/paintings/english-or-french-the-wilton-diptych

CRUSADES – BALKANS – DIGESTIVE & SENSES – RELIGIOUS ART

Additional Layer
There is Islamic art out there, but it's not religious in the same way that Christian art is. Muslims believe that depicting the human form is idolatrous, so their art consists of geometric shapes and repeating patterns.

Islamic design, shared by dalberra under CC license.

Additional Layer
Leonardo da Vinci made his own bestiary. He loved to study, sketch, and write about biology. Besides studying and diagramming animals, he also studied human anatomy.

Book Project
Read *The Spiderwick Chronicles* by Tony DiTerlizzi and Holly Black. The story tells of a man named Spiderwick who makes a field guide of invisible creatures.

Make your own imaginary creature bestiary.

God)
- Halo (represents someone who was righteous)

EXPLANATION: Christianity, Islam, and Judaism
Religious art is not prevalent among all religions. It is mostly utilized among Christian sects. There are countless pictures, sculptures, and other pieces of artwork that depict Jesus Christ, scenes from the Bible, and other Christian motifs. Christians, for the most part, believe art to be inspiring and instructional. At times however, it has been controversial even among Christians. The commandment to not worship graven images is often cited, and at various times, like during the Reformation and the 8th century iconoclast movement, much of the sacred art belonging to the church was destroyed. Of course, many artists of those times fought against those ideas and continued to create religious art.

In distinct contrast to Christianity, Islamic and Jewish people have historically discouraged the creation of religious art. At times it has even been forbidden. If you pick up any anthology of art it is easy to see that Christianity has been the focus of the majority of the artwork throughout the ages.

☺ ☺ ☺ EXPLORATION: A Medieval Bestiary
A bestiary is a book of animals. They were made from ancient times, but were made popular in medieval times. They taught the idea that the entire world is the word of God, and that every living thing exists to teach us about God.

Each page of the book had an illustration of something in nature – mostly animals, but also rocks, trees, and other things of the natural world. Along with the picture, each page also contained a description of the animal, its characteristics and habits, and also a moral lesson. For example, a page about a butterfly might include a thought about how migrating butterflies always return home, just as we must all return to our heavenly home. A page about a lamb details how lambs can recognize the voice of their mother, even in a very large flock. We too, can recognize the voice of God. Parallels were drawn between the natural world and Christian beliefs.

35

CRUSADES – BALKANS – DIGESTIVE & SENSES – RELIGIOUS ART

Make your own bestiary. Use online how-to-draw tutorials to create five to ten pictures of animals. Look up some basic information about each animal's appearance, habitat, diet, and behaviors. Then try to draw a parallel between faith and the life of the animal and include it on the page. When all of your animal pages are complete, bind it into one book and write "Bestiary of _____" (fill in the blank with your name).

If you would like to peruse some of the text of actual bestiaries, check out this index of bestiary animal descriptions from the Medieval Bestiary:
http://bestiary.ca/beasts/beastalphashort.htm

☺ ☺ ☺ **EXPLORATION: Ancient and Medieval Art Timeline**
Print out the timeline page from the end of this unit. Cut each art event out and look up the dates of that art period. Some will be overlapping. Place it on the correct place on the timeline and glue it down.

Can you see any correlations between what was happening in the world and the art that was created? You may want to find other historical events to add to your timeline as well. Can you identify periods when Christianity played a bigger role in art? Put a star on the timeline that indicates the time of the life of Jesus Christ.

Fact or Fiction?
The medieval writers didn't always have their facts straight. For example, several sources said that bees were born from cattle. However, some observations they made were disregarded, then later proven scientifically – like the migration of birds.

Explanation
The timeline from this unit looks primarily at Western art, but there was art being created in other parts of the world too. People from Asia, Africa, and the Americas all created art in ancient and medieval times as well. We just tend to focus on European art because it is the ancestor art of our civilization.

Coming up next . . .
Unit 2-10
Burgundy, Venice, & Spain
Switzerland
Nerves – Oil Paints

Crusades – Balkans – Digestive & Senses – Religious Art

My Ideas For This Unit:

Title: _____ Topic: _____

_____
_____
_____
_____
_____
_____
_____
_____

Title: _____ Topic: _____

_____
_____
_____
_____
_____
_____
_____
_____

Title: _____ Topic: _____

_____
_____
_____
_____
_____
_____
_____
_____

CRUSADES – BALKANS – DIGESTIVE & SENSES – RELIGIOUS ART

My Ideas For This Unit:

Title: _____ Topic: _____

_____
_____
_____
_____
_____
_____
_____
_____
_____

Title: _____ Topic: _____

_____
_____
_____
_____
_____
_____
_____
_____
_____

Title: _____ Topic: _____

_____
_____
_____
_____
_____
_____
_____
_____

Crusaders

Crusaders were Christians who joined the cause to fight against heathens. Most of them went to the Holy Land where they fought against Muslim armies, who had been attacking Christians and destroying Christian churches and holy sites for years. They were sincere believers and were defending not only their faith, but their nations from the incursions of Islam and its holy wars.

Layers of Learning

Crusades: Unit 2-9

1065
Westminster Abbey consecrated

Nov 27, 1095
Pope Urban II calls for a Crusade

1096-1099
First Crusade

June 1097
Crusaders take Antioch

July 15, 1099
Crusaders capture Jerusalem

1099
Knights Hospitaller founded

1119
Knights Templar Founded

1147-1149
Second Crusade

1163
Notre Dame Cathedral construction begun

Oct 3, 1187
Saladin Captures Jerusalem

1189-1192
Third Crusade

Oct 4, 1190
Teutonic Knights founded

1191
King Richard I of England goes on Crusade

July 12, 1191
Crusaders capture Acre

Dec 11, 1191
Richard captured by a German Baron near Vienna and held for ransom

Mar 3, 1193
Death of Saladin

Mar 12, 1194	Mar 28, 1194	1201-1204	1205
Richard returns to England to find John has usurped his kingdom	Richard captures Nottingham Castle, retaking his kingdom	Fourth Crusade	St. Francis of Assisi founds Franciscan order of Friars
1218-1221	**1228-1229**	**1233**	**1248-1254**
Fifth Crusade	Sixth Crusade	Inquisition begun in Germany	Seventh Crusade
1270	**1304**	**1309**	**1311**
Eighth Crusade	Divine Comedy written by Dante	Knights Hospitaller take over the island of Rhodes and make it their base	Knights Templar disbanded; members burned at the stake
1344	**1345-1350**		
Plague in Constantinople	Plague spreads across Europe		

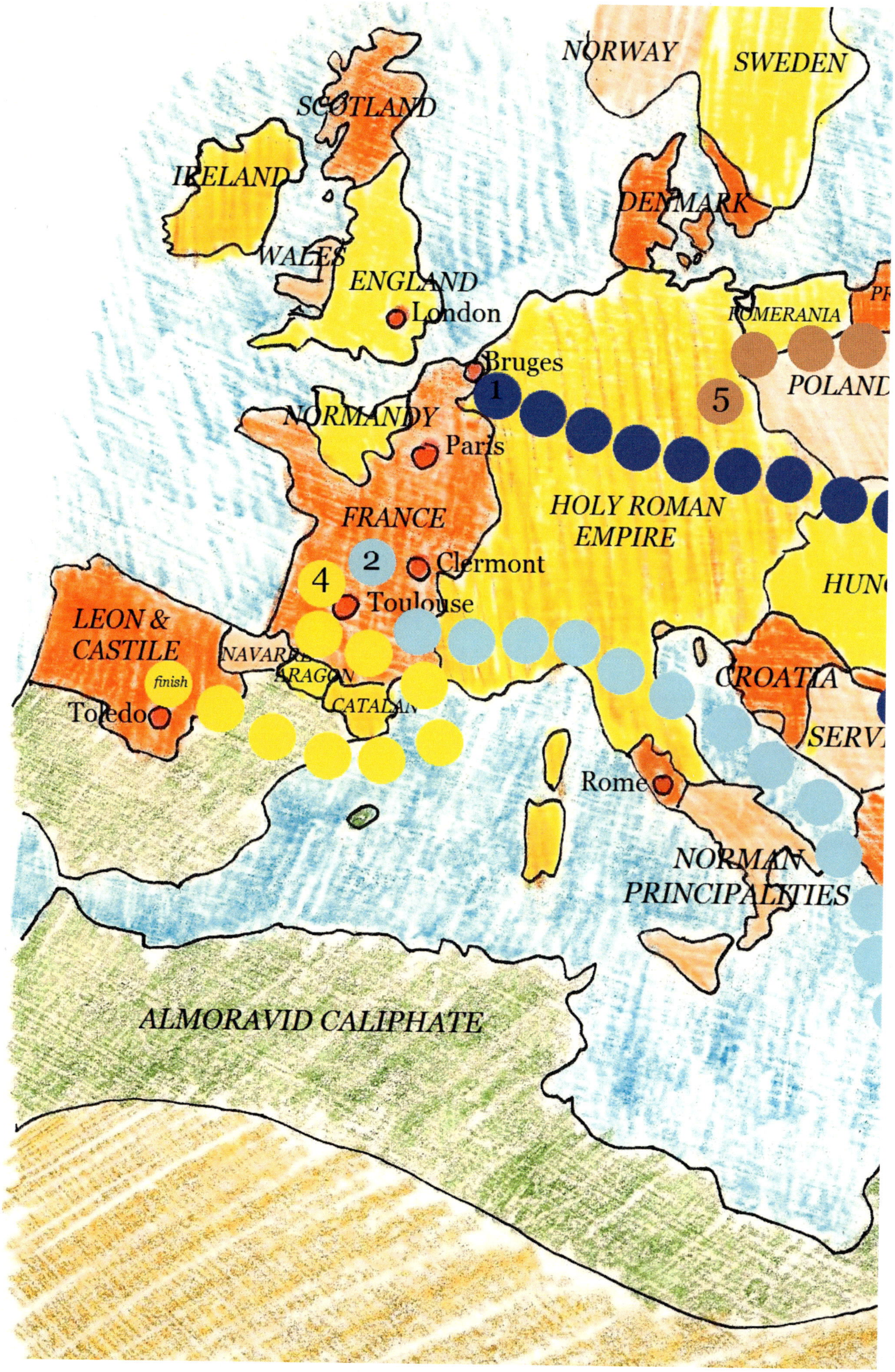
NORWAY
SWEDEN
SCOTLAND
IRELAND
DENMARK
WALES
ENGLAND
London
POMERANIA
Bruges
1
5
POLAND
NORMANDY
Paris
FRANCE
HOLY ROMAN EMPIRE
2
Clermont
4
Toulouse
LEON & CASTILE
NAVARRE
ARAGON
CATALAN
finish
Toledo
CROATIA
Rome
NORMAN PRINCIPALITIES
ALMORAVID CALIPHATE

Crusaders & Kings

Outremer

ESTONIA
LITHUANIA
PRUSSIA
RUSSIA
PECHENEGS
HUNGARY
SERVIA
BYZANTINE
GREAT SELJUK EMPIRE
ARMENIANS
FATIMID CALIPHATE
ARABIA

Constantinople
Nicaea
Ephesus
Adalia
Rhodes
Crete
Cyprus
Edessa
Antioch
Acre
Ascalon
Jerusalem

Go to 3
finish

These are the cards for the peasant crusaders who start at Bruges, the dark blue trail. Print the cards onto card stock, dark blue if you have it, and cut them apart. Draw the cards and move as directed.

1 Peter the Hermit is gathering people in Cologne, you decide to join him, move **back three spaces** while you wait for everyone to gather.	**1** Everyone has gone crazy. They're killing Jews in every town they find them. You thought this Crusade was going to be about Muslims in Jerusalem, not Jews in Europe. You hurry forward and skip the violence. Move **ahead three spaces.**	**1** No one in Peter's Army has any food. Most of the people are completely indigent. Go **back two spaces** while you scour the countryside for something to eat.	**1** Dozens of people die every day from starvation, disease, exhaustion, and exposure. Go **back two spaces** to help bury the dead.
1 You decide to go with some of the others by boat along the Danube river for part of the trip. Move **ahead three spaces**.	**1** At the town of Zamun an argument over the price of a pair of shoes turns into a brawl and then into a riot and from there into a full scale invasion. The whole army is delayed for a week while they pillage. Go **back three spaces**.	**1** Everyone is cheerful and excited about what is ahead. Move **ahead five spaces.**	**1** You've made a couple of really good friends along the way, people who are passionate about the cause like you are. Move **ahead five spaces**.
1 The commander of Nis, wanting just to get the mob of so called crusaders out of his territory promises escort and food clear to Constantinople. Move **ahead four spaces.**	**1** Some idiots burned a mill along the road, the situation got out of hand and nearly 10,000 of the crusaders in your company were killed. You had been traveling ahead of the company and so missed the violence, move **ahead three spaces**.	**1** You're not sure you can take any more of the craziness of this Crusade, but you're an awfully long way from home now. If you stay with the crusaders move **ahead two spaces**. If you join the Teutonic Knights **move to the brown 5** space.	**1** Everyone is cheerful and moving right along in spite of hardships. Move **ahead three spaces**.
1 The burghers of the town gave your company provisions if you would just keep moving on. This is the first time you've been full in weeks. Move **ahead four spaces**.	**1** A company of several thousand real knights from France led by Walter Sans-Avoir left you, not wanting to travel with the rabble. You're very worried but the company forges **ahead four spaces.**	**1** When you get to the town of Belgrade you realize those suits of armor hanging on the city walls belonged to Walter, the leader of the body of knights that was supposed to be ahead of you. You have to stop to avenge Walter. Go **back one space**.	**1** So many people have died that even though it's cold you have plenty of clothes, stolen from the corpses, to keep you warm at night. Move **ahead two spaces**.

These are the cards for the Knight Crusaders who start at Clermont, the light blue trail. Print the cards onto card stock, light blue if you have it, and cut them apart. Move as directed.

(2) Just today you sewed a red and white cross of the order of the Hospitallers to your shoulder. It shows that you are part of their cause. You're very proud. Move **ahead three spaces**.

(2) You've finally found a knight who will accept you as a squire. His name is Tancrede, he is the nephew of a knight from Southern Italy, Bohemond of Taranto. His squire died and he agreed to take you on. Move **ahead five spaces**.

(2) Your company was able to stop at a minor sacred site and pray over the relics of St. Paul himself. Move **back one space** because you are delayed.

(2) You're cooling your heels for a month waiting for the commander to arrange a ship to take your company across the Mediterranean. Go **back three spaces**.

(2) You pass into land where the crops and homes have all been burned, no people, only corpses. Rumor says it was done by a neighboring baron. You see why Urban urged the fighting men to war against the real enemy instead of their own people. You get new resolve, move **ahead five spaces**.

(2) You pass a group of peasants, each with a small white cross sewn on the shoulder of his or her tunic. You shake your head, they will never even make it to Constantinople. Move **ahead three spaces**.

(2) You've never been to sea before and you find it is not at all nice, you're terribly sea sick. Move **back one space**.

(2) You're joined by a couple thousand knights from Italy. Move **ahead four spaces**.

(2) A pirate ship is sighted on the horizon. They won't harm your flotilla but the captain puts on a little more sail anyway. Move **ahead four spaces**.

(2) Another squire, Thomas, told you how the Knights Hospitalers had been fighting the Muslims for years. The story of the destruction of the pilgrim hospitals fills the time. Move **ahead three spaces**.

(2) Your master beat you for not knowing how to take care of his equipment. Your friend Thomas is teaching you and you learn quick. Move **ahead three spaces**.

(2) A storm at sea drives you back. You're pretty sure you're going to die. Move **back two spaces**.

(2) You overheard some of the knights talking about how they plant o become wealthy off plunder in the Holy Land. You're a little disappointed. Most knights are there for God, but not all. Move **back one space**.

(2) The knights are paying their way to Jerusalem, some having sold all they owned, so you pass through towns and ports quickly without incident. Move **ahead four spaces**.

(2) Ten years ago the Spanish had taken the city of Toledo from the Muslims and now news had reached your company that they were calling for more soldiers. If you decide to join the Crusade in Spain **move to the yellow 4**, otherwise **move ahead two**.

(2) You saw the city of Rhodes, the fortress of the Knights Hospitallers and the defense of the west, for the first time. Move **ahead three spaces**.

These are the cards for the Teutonic Knights who start at the yellow 5.

(5) You're in your first fight against the pagan Prussians. You're slightly wounded but you survive and you won the battle. Move **ahead four spaces**.	(5) One of the knights said that if the Prussians captured you they would roast you alive in your armor. You train twice as hard and vow never to be captured. Move **ahead three spaces**.	(5) In a town in Sambia you watch as hundreds of villagers line up for baptism. You know their only other option was death, but you're comforted that their souls will be saved. **Move ahead three**.	(5) There is an uprising in a town ahead, a place that you thought had accepted Christianity. You hurry to help put it down. Move **ahead four**.
(5) You thought when you joined with the Teutonic knights that you would be fighting, but most of the order are monks who tend gardens and run hospitals. You think maybe when this campaign is over you'll become a gardener. Move **ahead three**.	(5) You're working very hard learning to use weapons, taking care of the knights equipment and tending animals. You're very sore and tired. Move **back two spaces**.	(5) You're sent to a nearby monastery to train for a year before you can rejoin the campaign. Move **back three spaces**.	(5) You pass a village. The people stare at you with dead eyes. Your friend tells you they're Christian now so you don't have to fight against them anymore. You wonder and **move back one space**.

These are the cards for the Spanish Crusade, the Reconquista, that starts at the yellow 4.

(4) You found out that El Campeador, the greatest warrior in Spain, is now in Toledo and will be leading the crusaders. You're guaranteed to win now! Move **ahead two spaces**.	(4) News just arrived that the Kingdom of Navarre and the Kingdom of Aragon, two Christian kingdoms, were at war. It's not your fight, you'll have to go around the war zone. Go **back three spaces**.	(4) You just got news that some of the Muslim kingdoms on the peninsula were fighting among themselves. That will help your cause. Move **ahead four spaces**.	(4) You pass a caravan of families with carts. You find out they are settlers going to live in reconquered lands that were abandoned by the defeated Muslims. Move **ahead three spaces**.
(4) You're set upon by bandits in the hills. No one is killed, but a few of the members of your company are injured. You hurry ahead to get out of the mountains. Move **ahead three spaces**.	(4) You just heard the pope promised the crusaders in the Reconquista the absolution of their sins just like the crusaders to the Holy Land. You are relieved. Move **ahead three spaces**.	(4) The Knights Templar have just been ordered to join the fight in the Iberian Peninsula. You've always wanted to join one of the militant orders. Maybe this is your chance. Move **ahead two spaces**.	(4) You had no idea how hot it would be here. You're wiped out. Go **back three spaces**.

These are the cards for the Crusaders who made it to Constantinople, the orange trail. Print the cards onto card stock, orange if you have it, and cut them apart. Move as directed.

---

(3) At the siege of Nicaea you were wounded, not in battle, but while pushing ships across the land on log rollers to launch them in the lake behind the town. You have to stay behind while you heal. Go **back three spaces**.

---

(3) You keep hoping that Alexios of Byzantium will send his troops to join your cause, but you wait in vain. He never comes. Go **back one space.**

---

(3) Everyone is in high spirits. Stephen of Blois wrote his wife, Adela, that the company would be in Jerusalem in five weeks. Move **ahead four spaces.**

---

(3) You get word that the Norman half of the army was under attack by Arslan the Turk. You hurry ahead, combine your two armies and the Turks flee. Move **ahead five spaces**.

---

(3) There is not enough food. The Turks are burning everything in your path before you even get there so the army has to range far and wide to find supplies. Go **back three spaces.**

---

(3) There are two many leaders. Everyone had expected Alexios of Byzantium to lead the combined forces. When he refused that left no one and everyone in charge. There are a lot of arguments. Move **back two spaces**.

---

(3) The peasants are really suffering, there is not enough food and water. It is hot. Horses and people die every day. There is a trial of death behind you. Move **back two spaces.**

---

(3) You sat outside the walls of Antioch for eight months laying siege to the city. There was no hope of defeating the walls, but finally a traitor was bought and the city fell. Move **ahead four spaces.**

---

(3) The leaders fight among themselves and delay the crusade for almost a year. Stephen of Blois, one of the most prominent leaders left to return to Europe. Move **back two spaces.**

---

(3) The march down the coast of the Levant goes very quickly as towns and cities surrender without a fight. There is more food now and the march goes quickly. Move **ahead four spaces.**

---

(3) There are very few peasants left from the original Crusaders who started out in Cologne. The few who are left have become slaves or servants to the Knights. It does speed up progress though. Move **ahead three spaces.**

---

(3) A ship from Genoa arrived with skilled engineers and timber to build siege engines with which to attack the city of Jerusalem. Move **ahead four spaces.**

---

(3) You caught sight of the city of Jerusalem gleaming in the late afternoon sun. Your eyes fill with tears. Move **ahead four spaces.**

---

(3) A ship arrived from Venice just in time to resupply the troops. Move **ahead four spaces.**

---

(3) Peter Bartholomew, a respected monk, discovers the Holy Lance in the city of Antioch. It gives everyone renewed hope and assurance that the cause is just. Move **ahead three spaces.**

---

(3) A combined army of Muslims dissolves when the Fatimids desert the Turkish leader, not trusting him. You defeat the Muslims without a fight. Move **ahead three spaces.**

These are the finish cards. Draw one after you get to a finish space to see what happens to you next.

You die in the siege of the city during the assault on the northern wall when a rock is dropped on your head. But the city was taken and the Pope had promised absolution so you're all right.	You live the rest of your life far from home as a servant to a knight. It's a hard life, but a good one.	You end up joining a militant order, becoming highly trained and dangerous with a sword. You live out your life as a soldier of God.	After your mission is finished you make your way home and live out the rest of your life as a farmer on your lord's lands. In your old age you tell your grandchildren stories of the crusades and make each of them promise never to go.
You stay until the mission is fulfilled but on the way home you're robbed and killed by bandits in the hills. No one ever knows what became of you.	You decide you've had enough of fighting and once the campaign is over you settle down as a monk in a quiet monastery and learn to raise herbs for healing.	You are badly wounded in the final attack and hover for weeks between life and death. Eventually you succumb to your wounds and the fever and infection that wracked your body and you are buried in sight of your goal.	You live through the battle without a scratch, but a few weeks later while part of a caravan to get supplies you're attacked and captured by Muslims. You become a slave and send the rest of your life serving those you fought against.

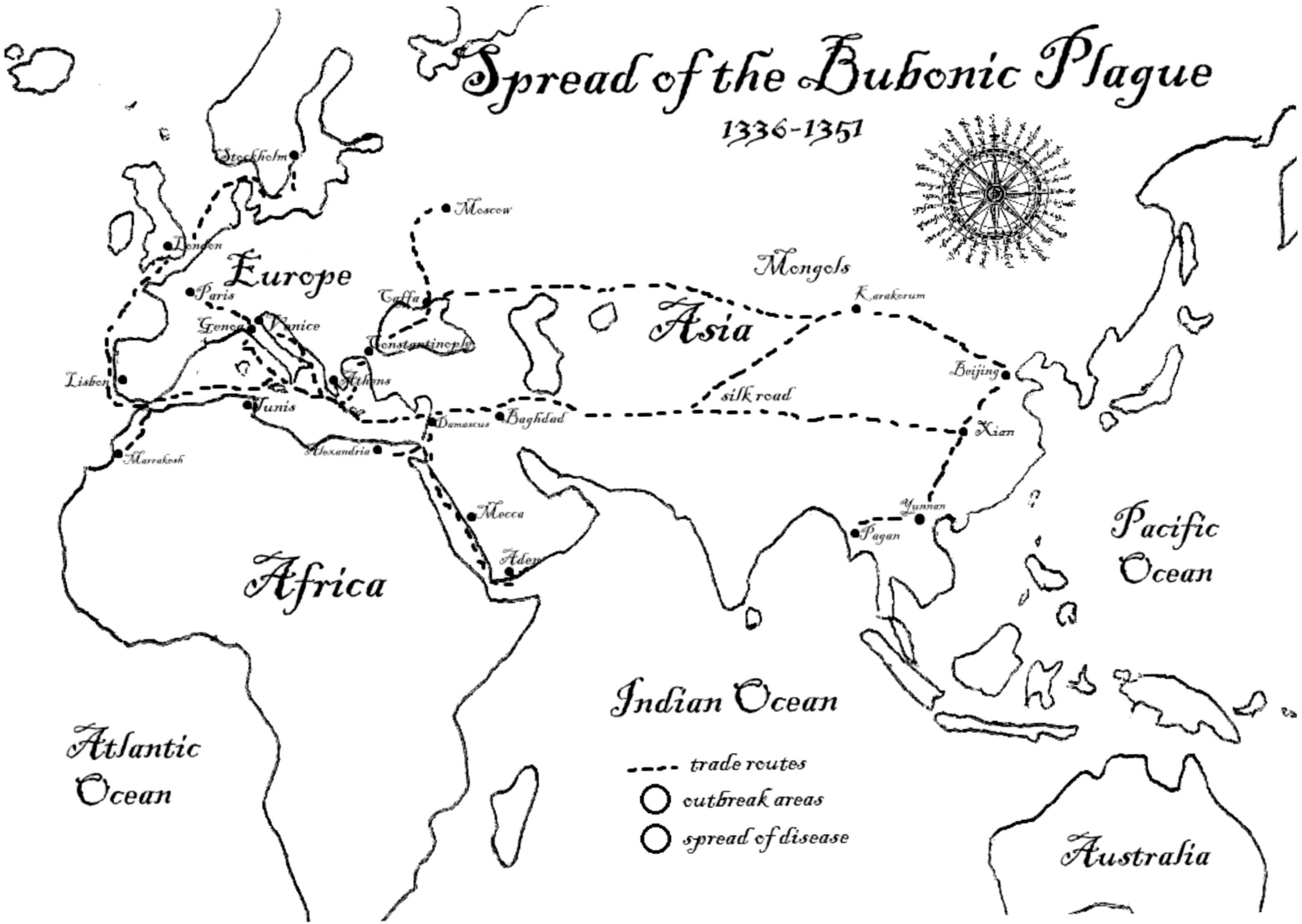
Spread of the Bubonic Plague
1336-1351
Stockholm
London
Europe
Paris
Genoa
Venice
Lisbon
Tunis
Marrakesh
Moscow
Caffa
Constantinople
Athens
Damascus
Baghdad
Alexandria
Mecca
Aden
Africa
Mongols
Karakorum
Asia
silk road
Beijing
Xian
Yunnan
Pagan
Pacific
Ocean
Indian Ocean
Atlantic
Ocean
trade routes
outbreak areas
spread of disease
Australia

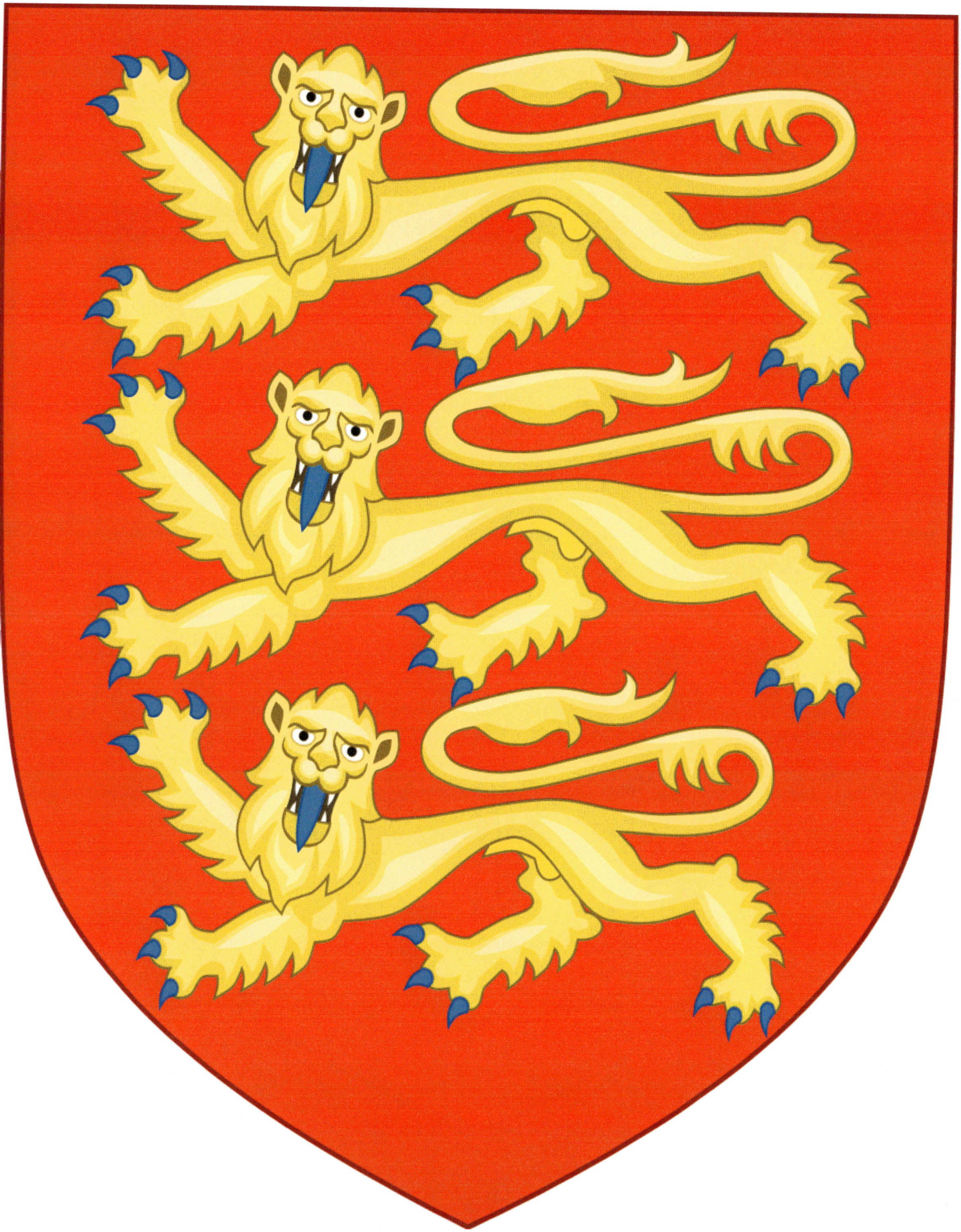

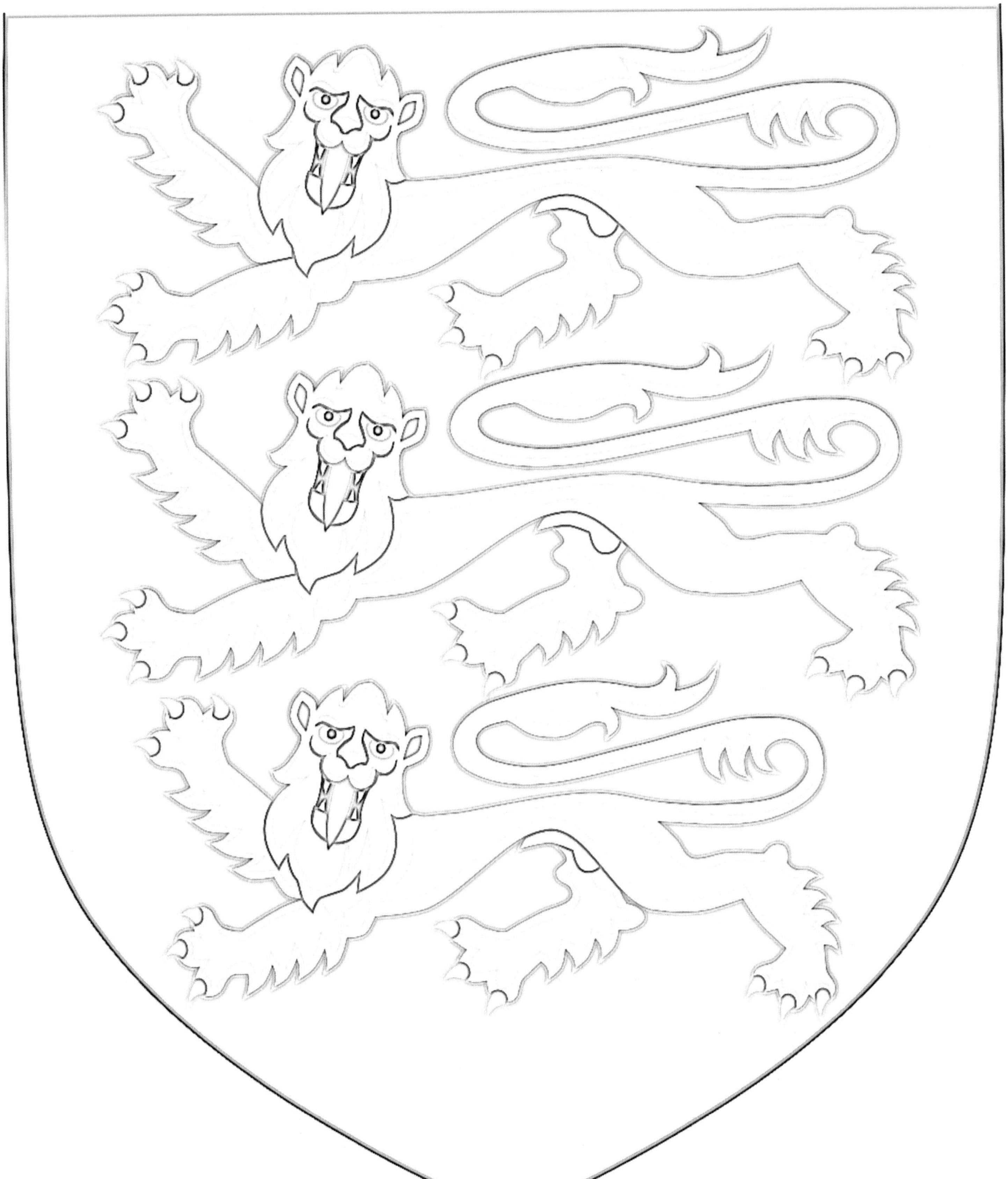

Balkan States

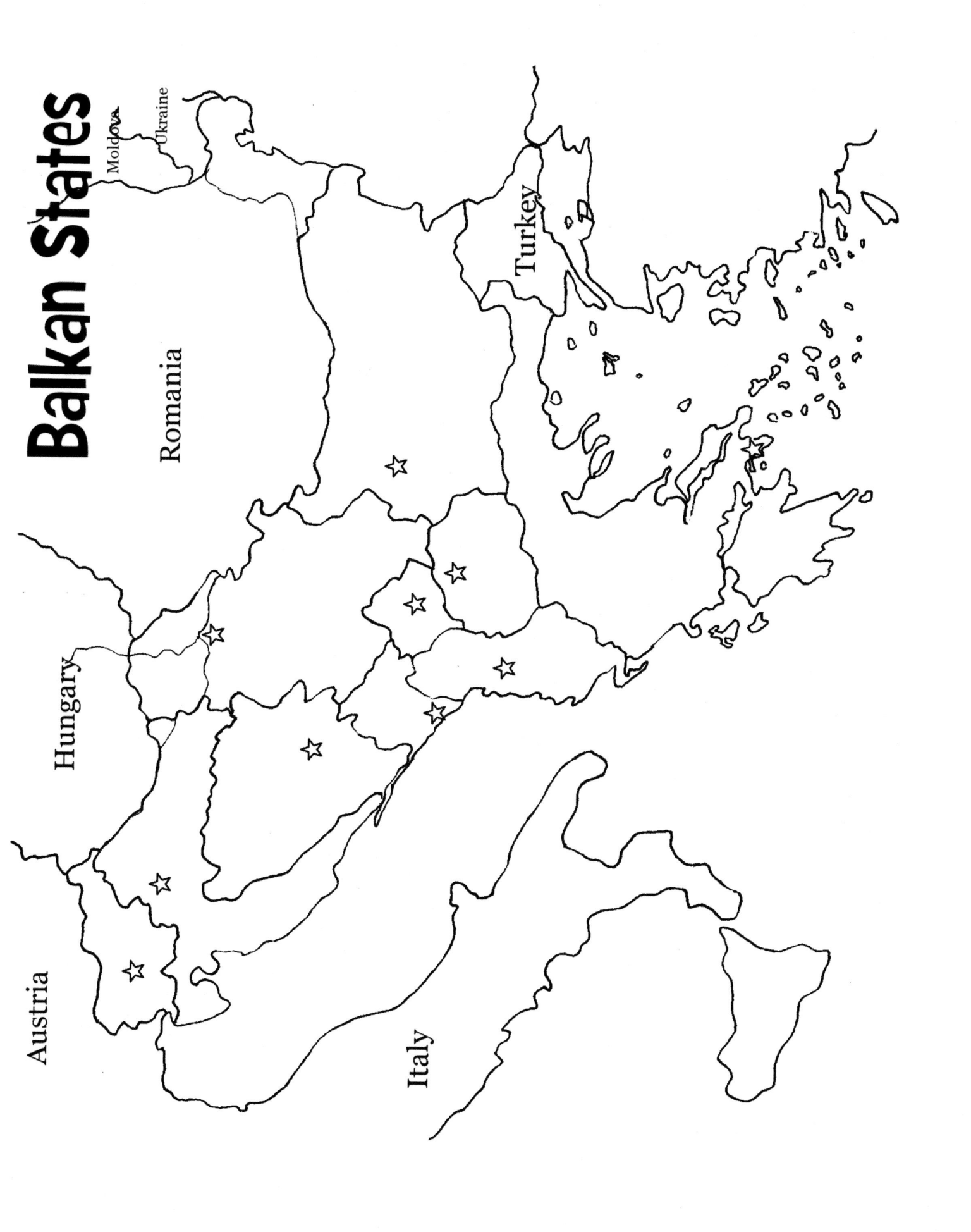

Moldova
Ukraine
Romania
Turkey
Hungary
Austria
Italy

Travel Brochure

(name of place)

Fun Things To Do!

-
-
-
-
-

I would like to vacation here because....

Human Eye

Label the diagram of the eye. Here is a word bank to help you.

Optic Nerve   Pupil   Retina   Iris
Lens   Vitreous Fluid   Cornea

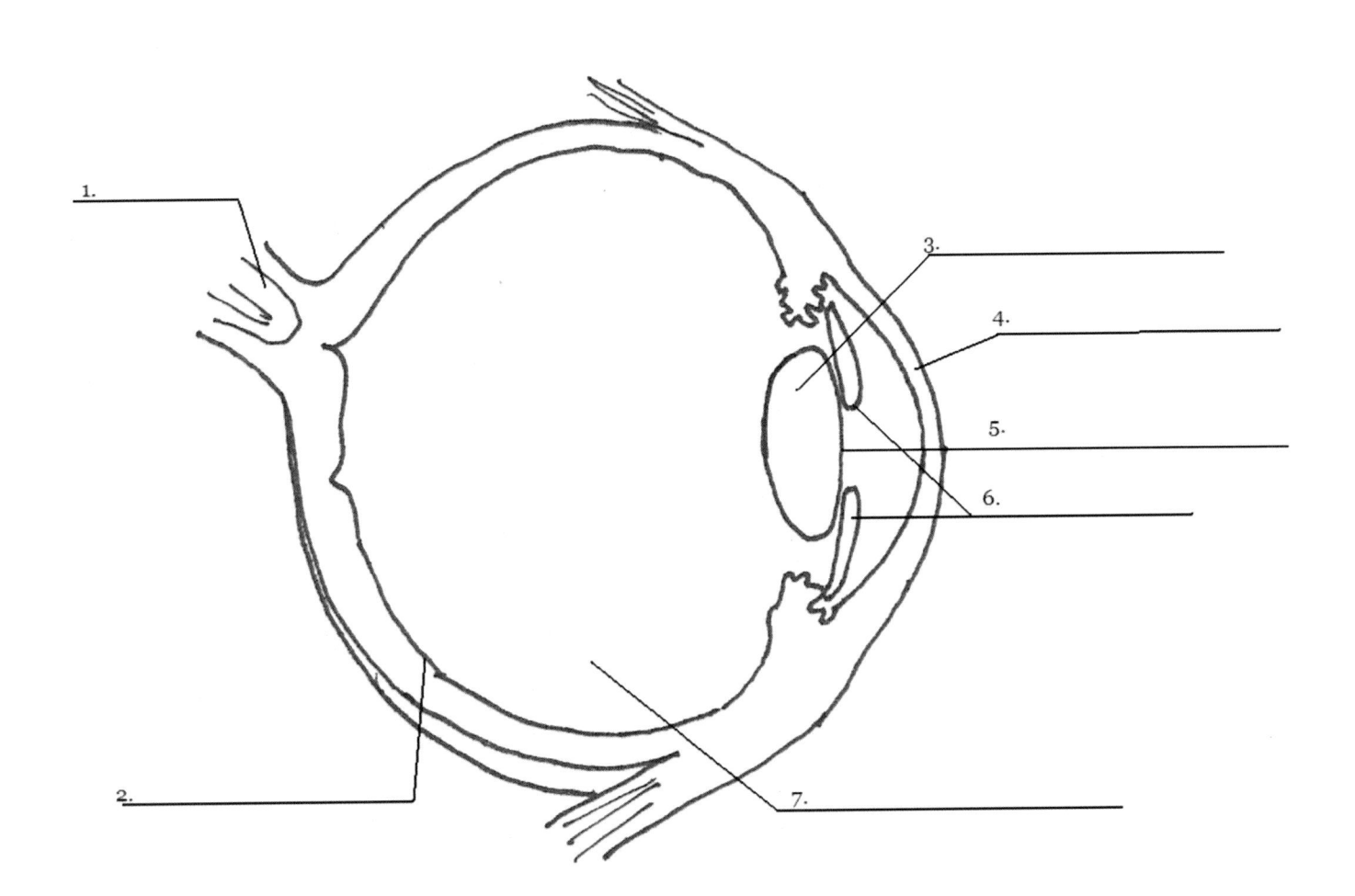

1.
2.
3.
4.
5.
6.
7.

Which part of the eye sends signals to the brain? _____

This is the part of your eye that is colored. _____

This is where the picture your eye sees is projected inside your eye. _____

Ancient and Medieval Art Timeline

Cut out the art events, look up their dates, and glue them correctly on the timeline below.

Timeline events (left side):
- 2500 — Great Pyramids built
- 2000
- Hammurabi's Code
- 1500
- 1000
- 500
- Peloponnesian Wars
- 0
- Fall of Rome
- 500 — Justinian rules
- Viking Raids
- 1000 — Crusades
- Columbus lands in New World
- 1500

Art events to place:
- Cave Painting
- Babylonian Art - Steles
- Ancient Egyptian Art and tomb paintings
- Classical Greek Art - focus on order, balance, and proportions
- Roman Art - imitated the Greeks
- Byzantine Art - mosaics were popular
- Iconoclasts destroy pictures and religious icons are banned
- Monks created illuminations
- Carolingian Art and spoilia from Rome
- Gothic Art and Architecture
- Beginning of the Renaissance

About the Authors

Karen & Michelle . . .
Mothers, sisters, teachers, women who are passionate
about educating kids.
We are dedicated to lifelong learning.

Karen, a mother of four, who has homeschooled her kids for more than eight years with her husband, Bob, has a bachelor's degree in child development with an emphasis in education. She lives in Utah where she gardens, teaches piano, and plays an excruciating number of board games with her kids. Karen is our resident Arts expert and English guru {most necessary as Michelle regularly and carelessly mangles the English language and occasionally steps over the bounds of polite society}.

Michelle and her husband, Cameron, homeschooling now for over a decade, teach their six boys on their ten acres in beautiful Idaho country. Michelle earned a bachelor's in biology, making her the resident Science expert, though she is mocked by her friends for being the *Botanist with the Black Thumb of Death*. She also is the go-to for History and Government. She believes in staying up late, hot chocolate, and a no whining policy. We both pitch in on Geography, in case you were wondering, and are on a continual quest for knowledge.

Visit our constantly updated blog for tons of free ideas,
free printables, and more cool stuff for sale:
www.Layers-of-Learning.com

Made in the USA
Columbia, SC
27 October 2021